Making the Most of Your Relationships

How to find satisfaction and intimacy with family and friends

WILLIAM STEWART

How To Books

Published by How To Books Ltd,
3 Newtec Place, Magdalen Road,
Oxford OX4 1RE, United Kingdom.
Tel: (01865) 793806.   Fax: (01865) 248780.
email: info@howtobooks.co.uk
http://www.howtobooks.co.uk

British Library Cataloguing in Publication Data.
A catalogue record for this book is available from
the British Library.

Edited by Diana Brueton
Cover design by Shireen Nathoo Design
Cover image PhotoDisc

Produced for How To Books by Deer Park Productions
Typeset by Dorwyn Ltd, Rowlands Castle, Hants
Printed and bound by Cromwell Press, Trowbridge, Wiltshire

NOTE: The material contained in this book is set out in good
faith for general guidance and no liability can be accepted
for loss or expense incurred as a result of relying in particular
circumstances on statements made in this book. The laws and
regulations are complex and liable to change, and readers should
check the current position with the relevant authorities before
making personal arrangements.

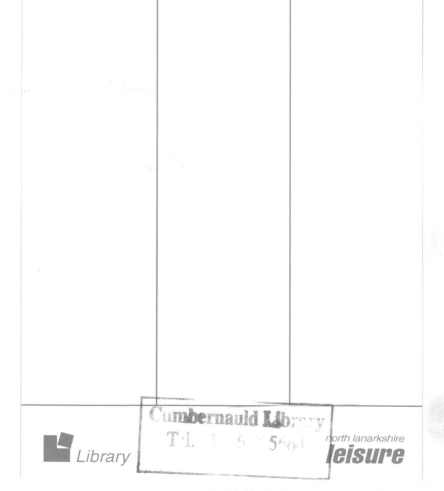

Books to change your life and work.
Accessible, easy to read and easy to act on –
Other titles in the **How To** series include:

Going for Counselling
Discover the benefits of counselling and which approach is best for you

Dating, Mating and Relating
The complete guide to finding and keeping your ideal partner

Self-Counselling
How to develop the skills to positively manage your life

Achieving Personal Well-Being
How to discover and balance your physical and emotional needs

When What You've Got is Not What You Want
Use NLP to create the life you want and live it to the full

The **How To** series now contains
around 200 titles in the following categories:

Business & Management
Career Choices
Career Development
Computers & the Net
Creative Writing
Home & Family
Living & Working Abroad
Personal Development
Personal Finance
Self-Employment & Small Business
Study Skills & Student Guides

Send for a free copy of the latest catalogue to:

How To Books
3 Newtec Place, Magdalen Road
Oxford OX4 1RE, United Kingdom
email:info@howtobooks.co.uk
http://www.howtobooks.co.uk

Contents

Preface

To be in a relationship means to be involved, connected. This book explores some ideas of how to build and maintain relationships. Because we are all engaged in relationships, from the cradle to the grave, it is a subject which is not often written about.

We can think about **primary relationships** – with parents, siblings, spouse, children – where there is emotional involvement; or **secondary relationships** – those that are more casual, with people we meet only occasionally, and with whom we do not have deep emotional contact. Yet both primary and secondary relationships have a vital function in life, and each presents its own difficulties and rewards, and each demands of us different skills if we are to make them work.

'If we are to make them work' begs the question, 'How can we make relationships work?' Some might argue that there is nothing they or anyone else can do; either the relationship works or it doesn't. This book will argue that there is much that we can all do to enhance any relationship. However, it has to be said that for any relationship to work and to be satisfying, making it work does not rest with one person. If the other person does not want the relationship to work, then it will not develop or it will cease.

This book is not a blueprint for successful relationships; there is no such thing. If you want to understand more about relationships, this book will challenge you to rethink some of your ideas about yourself and other people. It will help you to develop your ability to deal with people.

It would be arrogant and presumptuous of me to even think that I have all the answers: I don't. No one person does. However, having worked with relationships for the best part of my life, I have learned a great deal of what makes relationships work, and what hinders effective relationships.

It is essential to note that effective relationships does not mean 'perfect'. There is no such state as the perfect relationship. Many people chase that particular elusive butterfly, and never catch it. This book deals with reality. Relationships can be healthy and satisfying, even though at times they are stormy. Others can be disastrous, where there is constant war. That, too, is reality.

If you know that getting on with people is not your forte, then there is something you can do about it. You don't need to live another day with the knowledge that you act like a Jonah on people. You can change the way you relate to people. That change will benefit you, as well as other people. Remember, if you don't establish and maintain effective relationships, everybody suffers. This book is for you; for us all. We can all learn how to enhance our relationships.

William Stewart

1

Getting the Most from this Book

Books can be read for entertainment, or for instruction, which includes personal development. Being a self-help book this is a cross between instruction and self-development. Its main purpose is to help you build relationships. Here are some hints to help you get the most out of the book.

APPLYING WHAT YOU READ

Throughout the book keep asking yourself, 'How does this apply to me, to my situation?' In this way you will read with under-standing and purpose. Indeed without this self-application it is unlikely that what you read will make much lasting impression. As a writer I have to try to develop a relationship with you, the reader, in much the same way that any relationship is established and maintained. As you ask yourself 'How does this apply to me, to my situation?' you are reaching out to me, and listening to what I have to say; trying to understand why I have said some-thing in this particular way. The relationship between writer and reader is imperfect, because it is one-way; I cannot hear what you have to say, there is no feedback. However, taking that limitation into account, there are several things you can do to enhance what you read.

CHALLENGING WHAT YOU READ

Do not take everything I say as gospel. Challenge it. Criticise it. Say, 'This is not for me.' But don't reject it out of hand. Think through why you are discarding it:

- Does what I say challenge you too much?
- Do you find it offensive, if so, why?
- Does it not apply to your situation?

- If it doesn't apply fully, does it in part?
- How could you adapt what I have said so that it is more pertinent to you and your situation?
- If you and I could have a conversation, what would you want to say to me on that particular issue?

One way you can make up for this lack of contact with me is to write it down, or even record it on tape. In this way you will add to your self-awareness, and if in so doing your relationships with other people become more satisfying, then your work has been worthwhile.

TAKING TIME TO ABSORB THE IDEAS

If you were reading a novel you would probably read through each chapter fairly rapidly, moving forward, eager to find out what the principal character was up to next. Certainly you may do this with this book, but you are the principal character, not me, not the handsome, rich Lord Wellbethought, who is intent on capturing the love of the ravishing beauty. Just as a clever novelist develops the character gradually – you don't learn everything about him in the first chapter – so with this book. The book is progressive, and in this way your understanding will develop gradually. Take time to absorb the material.

CHECKING YOUR UNDERSTANDING FREQUENTLY

When you reach the end of a chapter ask yourself, 'What did I learn from that? What lessons can I take with me into the next chapter? What lessons can I take with me into the world of relationships? How can I adapt this to my situation?'

Work through the exercises and case studies
Take time to work through the exercises. Then think how you might apply the principles. Examine the case studies and think how they apply, or do not apply, to you.

MAKE NOTES OF IDEAS

Read with a notebook to hand to record anything that appeals to you. You may want to mark something for further study. Some people hate making notes on a book, but a tiny number in the margin will guide your eye to a reference. Treat the book as a study guide or workbook. Devote space to recording your self-observations. Be specific. But be cautious; if you are writing about other people, or even about yourself, do you want other people to have access to what you write? If not, then keep your writing safe from prying eyes. Even the most trusted of people may be consumed by curiosity about what you are writing. On the other hand, being open about what you are writing, with the proviso that it is private, might be enough to avert curious eyes prying into your inner thoughts. One of the advantages of such a record is that you can look back on it and see the progress you have made.

As an author I find it necessary to read and reread what I have written, for by the time several chapters have been written the details of the first few are sometimes vague. That is why you might find it helpful to mark issues for review.

APPROACHING CHANGE GRADUALLY

Not everything in this, or any other, self-help book can be absorbed and put to use all at once. Remember, change takes place little by little. Be like a tree; let your leaves burst out slowly at the correct time. Given the right atmosphere you, too, will flourish. You have to create the atmosphere that encourages change.

This book can be a stimulus; it cannot create change. If there are things in your life you want to alter, then only you can do it. This book will encourage you to challenge the way you do things, the way you are. The rest is up to you. If one of your relationship traits is to heavily criticise, you have to determine to change that by trying to understand rather than criticise. If you find yourself constantly judging other people, then you can change that by trying to see things through their eyes. If your competitive spirit brings you into conflict with people, learning to be co-operative might be what will make a difference for you.

Listen to the underlying message

This book is not so much about absorbing information as hearing the underlying message. Just as a handful of people can look out of the same window and see something different, so no two people will hear the same message contained in this book. That is one of the things that will make the reading of this book exciting, discovering what you can take from the book to help you.

PUTTING THE IDEAS AND PRINCIPLES TO WORK

Relationships do not work in isolation. However much you may want to improve the way you relate to people, you will only judge how successful you are by making contact with people. Try to find someone to act as your trustee, someone to whom you can tell your hopes and dreams. Someone who will listen to your successes and failures, who will challenge you, encourage you, and whom you can **trust** to put up with you, because he or she loves you enough to believe in you.

CARRYING OUT REGULAR PROGRESS CHECKS

Related to the above is carrying out regular checks on how you are doing. When you have had an encounter with someone, consider how you feel.

Are you pleased with how you handled the situation? What went right for you?

If you feel dissatisfied, analyse what didn't go according to plan. What exactly are your feelings? Write your thoughts and feelings down. Maybe you can't identify more than a vague discomfort, a feeling out of sorts. Stay with that feeling. Something has upset the emotional balance. Run over the encounter again. Recreate the conversation, and try to identify what it is that now causes you to feel as you do. For example, did you say something to put the other person down, and that led to breaking off the conversation? Did the other person say something to put you down? Why did it have this effect on you? Did it touch a sore spot? What might you have done or said to generate the other person's response? This time of analysis need not be heavy, or time-consuming. It can be done as you go for a walk, lie in bed, or dig the garden.

Using drama to improve your performance

An excellent way to improve your awareness is by using a tape recorder. Recreate the encounter. Play both parts (or all parts if appropriate). Try to get all the facts and feelings in, with the innuendoes, as if you were recording a script for a play. Give the characters names and personalities. Create the dialogue, as much as you can remember.

You will find that the more you do this, the more accurate your recall will be. Play yourself, and be scrupulously honest with the words you used. Be again the person you were – angry, aggressive, whinging, sickly, sympathetic, over-solicitous and so on. Replaying it in this way will show you areas you could improve. If you are courageous enough, you might allow your trusted friend to hear what you have recorded.

> Improving the way we relate to people means changes, and change demands courage. Go for it!

2

Understanding What Relationships Mean

Relationships are not static; they are living and dynamic. They can be positive or negative, supportive or destructive, loving or hateful, caring or abusive. They come into existence, they flourish and they die. They do so because relationships are people. It is true that we develop relationships with animals, but this book is concerned with relationships between people.

IDENTIFYING PRIMARY AND SECONDARY RELATIONSHIPS

- **Primary relationships** are long-lasting, founded upon strong emotional ties and a sense of commitment to each other. Primary relationships are such that one member cannot simply replace the other with a new person. A primary relationship exists between parent and offspring.
- **Secondary relationships** are relatively short-lived relationships between people, characterised by limited interaction, clear rules for relating and well-defined social roles. They rarely have much in the way of emotional involvement, and the members in the relationship can be replaced rather easily. We have secondary relationships with neighbours, workmates and those with whom we join in specific activities, such as sport or church.

Secondary relationships are not unimportant; in fact, they can often have more meaning and be more rewarding than primary relationships. This find echoes in the old saying: You can't choose your relatives, but you can choose your friends.

GETTING ON WITH PEOPLE IS LIKE DRIVING A CAR

Getting on with people is like learning to drive a car. You can read all the books ever printed on how to be a super driver; you may know the Highway Code back to front and be able to answer all the questions, but until you get in the car and put your reading into practice, you will never move the car one metre. You may attend a driving school which puts you in a simulator, and that helps, but it is not the real thing *and you know it.*

Knowing what to do is different from actually doing it.

Your driving instructor will guide you through the settling-in routine, but until you engage the gears and let off the handbrake, you will stay put. Setting off from the kerb and entering the stream of traffic takes courage. As your lessons progress you will start to feel more confident, and from time to time your instructor will remind you of the rules of the road.

Getting on with people is something like that. We do not come into this world with a printed circuit board in our brains – how to get on with people and how to make a success of relationships. We learn by experience: some happy, some painful and disastrous.

If there is no blueprint, can we learn how to get on with people? The answer is yes we can. This book is not a blueprint, rather, it offers some guidelines as to what you can do to get on with people.

However it has to be said that no matter how understanding you are, however hard you try, however accommodating and pleasant, there are some people you will never get along with. That is the nature of people.

Relationship-building
We often talk of 'relationship-building,' and this is very much what relationships are – building and hard work. Some people are fortunate enough to have acquired the ability to get on with people early in life. For many of us, however, building relationships is hard work.

Expanding the analogy
In driving a car and getting on with people you:

- have to want to
- have to learn the rules
- have to work at it
- have to listen to the person alongside you

- build up your skill with experience
- will experience some near misses.

CONNECTING WITH PEOPLE

Dictionary definitions of relationships are vague, and most state the obvious – that a relationship is the position of people who are related. But that does not get beneath the surface, to what a relationship is. Although relationships may be multiple, for the sake of clarity only the relationship between two people will be considered in any depth.

For a relationship to come into existence and to continue, the two people must feel that they are connected. Connection implies something that joins two people. There are many analogies one could think of: telephone, railway lines, the internet. For the relationship to continue, the connection has to be kept clear of obstacles.

When a connection weakens

When a connection works loose, trouble ensues. We know this from the example of the telephone, or an electrical appliance. If a wire in my computer plug works loose, I am in trouble. If the tie in a relationship works loose, the relationship is in trouble. If the break in the connection is not repaired my computer will not work, or it will not be reliable. If the connection between two people weakens, and is not repaired, the relationship is unlikely to survive.

IDENTIFYING DIFFERENT TYPES OF RELATIONSHIPS

So far we have looked at some aspects of relationships, in order to arrive at some understanding of what the word means. One way to approach this is to say that a relationship exists when there is *any on-going association of two individuals.*

Examples of relationships are:

- sexual partners
- husband/wife
- parent/child
- teacher/pupil
- friendship

- family
- manager/worker.

Some relationships are intense, others are more casual. Some casual relationships we could live without; the more intense and personal the relationship, the more we would feel pain and loss if it ended.

Relationships have meaning, and as such they influence behaviour. The relationship between teacher and student is such that the behaviour of the one influences the behaviour of the other. It would be difficult to say with any degree of certainty which person *caused* the other to behave in a certain way. The same applies to the parent/child relationship. In a marriage, both partners influence each other's behaviour to the degree that very often they appear to be thinking the same and mirror each other. (Here I am using marriage to refer to any intimate and on-going relationship, even though the couple may not be legally married.)

Quality of relating

One of the characteristics of a relationship is that what goes on between people in a relationship is different from between people who are not in a relationship. This can be observed in what the two people do, but also in the quality of their interaction. Sometimes it is difficult to pinpoint exactly what that quality is, but keen observers can usually say when that certain quality is lacking. Generally the closer two people are, the more other people are able to detect the quality.

Exercise 2.1 Assessing your relationships

- Think of the relationships you had or still have.
- Which of the relationships do you value the most? Why?
- What was it that brought the relationship into being?
- How do you work towards keeping the relationship healthy?
- What does the other person do to keep the relationship healthy?
- What are the things that put strain on the relationship?
- If the relationship died, what caused the death?

Having worked through these questions, how do you feel about the particular relationship or relationships you had in mind as you did the exercise? Is there anything you could do to improve the relationship(s)?

CASE STUDY

Judy and Tom end their marriage

Tom came to me for counselling, wanting to talk about his marriage that was going wrong. He and Judy had been married for 12 years, and had two girls and one boy. Over the past year their marriage had been through a sticky patch – the connection had started to work loose. Judy had had an affair with a married man. Tom was caught up in establishing a new computer business.

Tom wanted to put the affair behind them and move forward. Judy agreed to come for counselling. When they arrived I was struck by their body language. They sat at opposite ends of the settee; they hardly looked at each other as they talked. But most striking of all was a marked lack of warmth in their language. They might have been two strangers meeting on a bus. The marriage ended in divorce.

Assessing the case study

This case study demonstrates an important principle: however willing one person is to make the relationship work, that is often not enough. A healthy relationship depends on the willingness of both people to make it work.

HANDLING MORE THAN ONE RELATIONSHIP

Although the emphasis of this book is on the one-to-one relationship, none of us exists only at that level. We have many relationships, some of which conflict with one another and make different demands on us.

For example, the couple with children have many different roles in life, and each with different relationships. But the principal roles of husband and wife might conflict with being parents. The relationship the wife has with her husband might conflict with the relationship she has with her own parents.

Thus every relationship we have places demands on all other relationships. Sometimes the **stress** between conflicting relationships can be so severe as to lead to the breakdown of one of them.

CASE STUDY

John can't separate from his mother

John had been married to Joan for two years. They were both in their mid-20s and lived about 30 miles from John's parents. The day they returned from their honeymoon John's mother, Alice, rang.

'You haven't let me know if you had a good honeymoon. You're not going to neglect your old mother, I hope!' She laughed, but it wasn't humorous. Neither was she old.

'Mother, we've only just got in,' said John.

'You still could have rung me. You know how I worry. Going all that way' (to Scotland).

John tried to pass it off, but he was angry. He began to feel trapped. If he didn't ring he knew Alice would be on the 'phone whinging. If he did ring, she would complain that he never visited her. Her jibe, 'Now you've got another woman in your life you don't care about me,' rankled. Joan tried to be friendly, but Alice was too possessive. John's dad, Bill, had long since opted out and hid behind his book or escaped to the garden shed. John and Joan bought an answering machine, hoping to get respite, but that only made things worse. Alice rang as much as 20 times in one day. In the end John accepted a job in Australia.

Assessing the case study
1 Alice found it impossible to let John lead his own life.
2 John's father would do anything for a quiet life.
3 John felt he was being sucked in by his mother and that he needed to break away.
4 It is difficult to see what John could have done to resolve the conflict. His mother seems to lack any insight and her own needs overwhelm her.
5 John's course of action might seem radical, but putting physical distance between him and his mother might be the only way he can achieve independence.

Exercise 2.2   Identifying conflicting relationships
As in the relationship between John and his mother, you may have relationships that conflict with each other.

The steps in this exercise are:

1 List all your relationships.
2 Decide if each of these is central to you, or fringe.
3 Decide which of these conflict with each other – how and why.
4 Try to work out a strategy (or strategies) for reducing the conflict.

Myself and other people
In the following questionnaire would you score yourself high, medium or low? Make a note of your score for each question.

In getting on with people I:
1 Build on their ideas.
2 Express warmth and affection.
3 Handle personal anger constructively.
4 Influence them positively.
5 Listen with understanding.
6 Receive warmth and affection.
7 Tolerate conflict and antagonism.
8 Tolerate views that conflict with my own.
9 Tolerate their behaviour.
10 Have aspirations of my own.
11 Am aware of my own feelings.
12 Am aware of their feelings.
13 Actively strive for self-awareness.
14 Enjoy close relationships.
15 Value their independence.
16 Value their creativity.
17 Am open-minded.
18 Show peace of mind.
19 Have physical energy.
20 Have high self-esteem/self-worth.
21 Can express myself.
22 Tolerate their differences from me.
23 Trust them.
24 Am versatile.
25 Am willing to discuss my own feelings.

Having completed this self-assessment, how would you sum up the way you get on with people? The more you have in the high section, the more satisfying your relationships are likely to be. If you have more in the medium and low sections do not despair, you have work to do. Take the items you scored in those two sections and work out how what you can do to move more into high. You might like to ask a close friend to assess you. You may find that someone else is kinder to you than you are to yourself. Let this be a valuable learning experience, not a put-down.

DEVELOPING SELF-AWARENESS TO ENHANCE RELATIONSHIPS

A fundamental premise of this book is that **self-awareness** is crucial to understand how to get on with people. A corollary of this is that the more we understand what makes people tick, the more effective relationships will be. The fact that we are involved in multiple relationships – family, marriage, friends, work – makes it imperative that we strive to understand the dynamics of relationships.

I wish it were feasible to say that understanding people results in perfect harmony. That is a pipe dream, without any basis in reality.

> Because we are unique, we respond to each other in different ways.

We are likely to respond with tenderness to a child who is crying, while we may feel embarrassment when a male companion breaks down in tears. We are likely to respond very differently to a person who is friendly than to one who is hostile and aggressive. Relationships are never static; when they are, they are either dying or are already dead. Because each relationship is uniquely different, we need to extend our awareness so as to cope more effectively.

SHOW ME HOW TO LIVE

A poem by an unknown author concludes this chapter. Although originally written for children, I have adapted it to apply to getting on with people. Getting on with children is one aspect of getting on with people generally, though it is by no means the same thing. Children make different demands on relationships than do adults, and vice versa.

Our children are the parents of the future. If, by the way we relate to them, we prepare them better for the task of parenthood, we will have added something of quality to society. They may look back and say, 'If only . . .' We should avoid giving them burdens they are not capable of carrying. We may not get it right. However, if we try to relate to them with all the qualities outlined in this lesson, we will have done all we are capable of.

I have given the original lines, with the adaptation alongside.

- If children live with criticism, they learn to condemn.
- If we criticise people, they will condemn us.
- If children live with hostility, they learn to fight.
- If we are hostile to people, they will fight us.
- If children live with ridicule, they learn to be shy.
- If we ridicule people, we destroy their self-worth.
- If children live with shame, they learn to be guilty.
- If we shame people, we increase their load of guilt.
- If children live with tolerance, they learn to be patient.
- If we are tolerant, people will be patient with us.
- If children live with encouragement, they learn confidence.
- If we encourage people, their confidence will be increased.
- If children live with praise, they learn to appreciate.
- If we praise people, they will appreciate themselves.
- If children live with fairness, they learn justice.
- If we are fair, people will not feel judged.
- If children live with security, they learn faith.
- If we offer security, people learn that we can be trusted.
- If children live with approval, they learn to like themselves.
- If we show approval, people will like themselves.
- If children live with acceptance, they learn to find love in the world.
- If we accept people as they are, they will be touched by our love.

SUMMARY

Relationships can be rewarding and incredibly satisfying. Or they can be the opposite, yet the majority of us cannot exist without them. Most of us need other people and they need us. Some relationships are positive; others are negative. Some relationships we could manage without, yet in some way all relationships help to meet some need within us. From the moment we are born we start to relate to people, and will go on doing so until we die.

Some people go through life encountering one disastrous relationship after another. Others, while they have their share of difficult relationships, manage to make a reasonable success of how they relate to people. People don't come into the world with an in-built gene called 'relationships' yet there is no doubt that within a few years of life some children are already adept at getting on with people. Other people grow up always seeming to be at loggerheads with others. These are the extremes; between are the majority of people.

Working towards change

Whatever your experience, however many disastrous relationships you have had, things can change if you want them to and if you are prepared to work towards change.

Of course, satisfactory relationships do not rest entirely with you. There are some people in this world who don't get on with anyone. However much you might want to build a relationship, that person is just not interested. In such a case probably the only answer is to cut your losses and get out. However, if you know in your heart of hearts that it is you who has the problem, then there is something you can do.

You do not have to become a saint, there are few of those around, but just changing one little bit of the way you relate to one person in your life can make a difference. Be like the baby taking his first steps. Learn to take the successes with the falls and in that way make progress. Decide today to make just one tiny change in the way you relate to someone. That might be your first step towards better relationships all round.

> You cannot change other people; you can only change yourself.

3

Working Towards Relationships that Satisfy

Healthy, positive, and satisfying relationships are major sources of well-being and high self-esteem. There is no blueprint for effective relationships. We all have to do the best we can in spite of our many limitations.

It could be argued that some people have 'people' gifts and qualities in dealing with relationships. Some people do seem to have natural relationship qualities, but they also have had to work hard to perfect those skills. An analogy may point home the message. The concert pianist of world-renown did not arrive there on talent alone; a great deal of dedication and hard slog were also necessary. Relationships are something like that. Relationships may not be your forte but you cannot help but be involved with people.

LEARNING ABOUT RELATIONSHIPS

Learning about relationships is one way of increasing self-esteem. For every point won we increase the 'self-esteem-o-meter', and the more energy we shall have to enjoy life, and other people will feel the benefit.

A relationship that does not satisfy will shrivel and die. One person can invest everything into establishing and making a relationship work, yet it may not survive. That is the painful truth. The more we invest in a relationship, the more pain results when the relationship breaks down. But for a relationship to work, to satisfy, there has to be investment, yet therein lies a snag. When we have been hurt by relationships that seemed to offer everything, only to find that they have died on us, the natural tendency is to draw back and so say: 'That's it! No more pain for me.' This chapter will examine some of the ingredients of satisfying relationships.

MAKING CONTACT WITH PEOPLE

The German/American psychoanalyst Karen Horney put forward her three-fold idea of how we relate to people.

1 *Moving toward.* The friendly type. Here we seek affection and approval.
2 *Moving against.* The aggressive type. Here we place heavy reliance on power.
3 *Moving away from.* The detached, private type. Here we seek to avoid dependency and conflict.

A danger of categorising people is that most of us at times could fit ourselves (and others) into these three types – *depending on the situation*. However, the point being made is that when we rely *exclusively* on one way of relating, then the others become subordinate, or even redundant. The friendly type can be so demanding of approval that they become clinging; the aggressive type can become a tyrant; the private type can become isolated and feel superior to others because they do not need people.

Exercise 3.1   Assessing your style of relating

You may find it helpful, after reading each question, to close your eyes and let your mind travel its own path.

In relation to each question also ask: Can you work out why? What feelings do you experience as you think about that person/those people?

1 In my current life and in my past life whom do I find myself moving towards or moving towards me?
2 In my current life and in my past life whom do I find myself moving against or moving against me?
3 In my current life and in my past life whom do I find myself moving away from or moving away from me?

You might not be able to do anything about relationships in your past life, but you can use the insights from this exercise to help you change relationships in the present.

UNDERSTANDING THE DIMENSIONS OF RELATIONSHIPS

From the above, three basic needs can be identified which influence relationships and help to keep our personality balanced:

- the need to be included
- the need to exercise control
- the need for openness.

Life is never perfect, but we can all strive towards a degree of balance. As we saw earlier, if any one of those basic needs gets out of control, it can lead to damage of ourselves as well as to other people.

Identifying the need to be included
- **Inclusion** is being *in* or *out* in relationships.
- Inclusion is concerned with achieving just the right amount of contact with people.
- Some people like a great deal of inclusion. They are outgoing, like to go to parties, doing things with a group, and start conversations with strangers.
- Other people prefer to be alone. They are more reserved, seldom start conversations and avoid parties.

Exercise 3.2   Assessing your need to be included
1 In which relationships do you feel included?
2 Which relationships would you like to feel included in but are not?
3 Which suits you better, to be outgoing or being on your own?

Identifying the need of control in relationships
- **Control** has to do with *top* or *bottom* in relationships.
- Some people are more comfortable being in charge of everyone. They like to be the boss, to give orders, to make decisions both for themselves and for others.
- Other people prefer to have no control over others. They are content never to tell people what to do. They even seek out situations where they have no responsibility.

Exercise 3.3   Assessing your control in relationships
1 In which relationships do you feel you are on top? Or on the bottom?
2 In which relationships would you like to feel on top but are not?
3 Would you rather have more control over others, or less?

Identifying openness in relationships
- **Openness** has to do with being *open* or *closed* in relationships.

- Some people enjoy relationships where they talk about their feelings, their secrets and their innermost thoughts. They enjoy having one person, or at most a few people, in whom they confide.
- Other people avoid being open. They prefer to keep things impersonal and have acquaintances rather than close friends.

Exercise 3.4   Assessing how open your relationships are
1 How open or closed are you in relationships?
2 In which relationships are you open?
3 In which relationships are you closed?
4 In which relationships are you able to talk about your feelings?
5 How would other people describe you, open or closed?

IDENTIFYING HOW AVAILABLE YOU ARE IN RELATIONSHIPS
This refers to being totally involved in whatever we are doing, with our total self.

- When we are low on **availability**, parts of us are scattered or detached. We are thinking of other things.
- When we are high on availability and identified with what we are doing, we may lose the sense of self as being different from what we are observing.

An analogy of availability would be watching a play, where it is essential to maintain emotional distance. To best experience a play we must be detached enough to know that it is *not* happening to us, yet not to be so coldly detached that it makes no impression.

Appropriateness means being capable of intense presence or intense detachment or anything in between.

Exercise 3.5   Assessing how available you are in relationships
1 Based on the section above, how do you make yourself available in relationships?
2 What can you identify as being the major issues that interfere with you being available, and why?
3 Can you identify any relationships in which you feel you are being taken over?
4 If the answer to question three was yes, how can you learn to be more detached, yet still be appropriately available?

IDENTIFYING HOW SPONTANEOUS YOU ARE IN RELATIONSHIPS

This refers to **spontaneous** expression.

- When we are low on self-control, we become *out of control* and sometimes behave in ways we later regret. Extreme spontaneity leads to wild and anti-social behaviour. People often use alcohol and drugs to release controls so that they will be more expressive or to increase their controls so that they will be calmer.
- When we are high on self-control, we feel inhibited and held back. We do not express ourselves fully. We become rigid and lack spontaneity. We are reluctant to take chances or risks for fear of what might happen.
- When we are appropriately spontaneous, we do what we wish to do and stop whenever we choose to. We are able to be totally free or totally controlled or anything in between depending on what is appropriate.

Being spontaneous is related to how much of our childhood we have retained.

Exercise 3.6   Assessing how spontaneous you are in relationships

1 In which relationships can you be spontaneous?
2 In which situations can you be spontaneous?
3 In which situations do you feel constrained and controlled?
4 How far were you encouraged as a child to be spontaneous?
5 If you feel you were too controlled as a child, how does this affect your behaviour now?

Exercise 3.7   Identifying how you relate to people

Once again you are invited to assess how you relate to people under: verbal expression; openness; tolerance; support; body language; and material evidence, or the actions we take. Select a particular relationship; it could be your spouse, partner, friend. Try to be as honest as you can be. Some of the questions might prove to be very challenging to answer truthfully.

(A)   Verbal expression
You tell each other never, occasionally, frequently:

1 That you feel you get along well together.
2 That you can talk to each other about anything.
3 That you trust each other completely.
4 That the thought of dying disturbs you.
5 That you feel you understand each other.
6 You don't have to put up a facade with each other.
7 That you have faith in each other.
8 That you are important to each other.

(B)   Openness
You tell each other never, occasionally, frequently:

1 The kind of behaviour in others that annoys you.
2 Whether or not you are thinking of making some major decisions in the near future.
3 Things about your personality that trouble you.
4 The chief health problems that cause you concern.
5 The major pressures about work.
6 Your worries and concerns about the future.
7 The things you are most sensitive about in relationships.
8 What, for you, is acceptable and not acceptable sexual behaviour.

(C)   Tolerance
You tell each other, or do for each other never, occasionally, frequently:

1 The things about each other's appearance that please you.
2 The things in your past you are ashamed about.
3 The problems you have with sex.
4 The things about each other you are proud of.
5 The things you do with, or for, each other.
6 Provide mutual support for personal activities.
7 Go places together because the other one would like to.
8 Sacrifice your own needs for the benefit of the other.
9 Show love by a willingness to change.

(D)   Support
What you do to support, encourage each other never, occasionally, frequently:

1 We trust each other and are truthful.
2 We listen to each other.
3 We approve of each other as people of worth.
4 We write to each other when we are separated.
5 We are considerate and not over-demanding of each other.
6 We show active and appropriate interest in each other's work.
7 We encourage each other to make our own decisions.
8 We are courteous to each other.

(E)   Body language
You demonstrate to each other never, occasionally, frequently:

1 That you want to be attractive for each other.
2 That you understand each other.
3 Continued affection.
4 You feel safe in each other's company.
5 That you miss each other when you are separated.
6 Courtesy, kindness and consideration.
7 Your admiration for each other.
8 How fortunate you are in your relationship.

(F)   Tender, loving, care
You demonstrate to each other never, occasionally, frequently:

1 We try to lift each other up when we are down.
2 We run errands for each other.
3 We are always ready to offer constructive suggestions.
4 We protect each other from harm.
5 We perform simple tasks for each other.
6 We help each other with various tasks.
7 We teach other skills the other doesn't have.
8 We pray for each other.

Assessing your answers
Discuss your answers with someone you trust; someone who knows you really well. It could be the person you had in mind when you answered the questions. Differences of opinion about certain statements could provide clues for a closer relationship.

CHARACTERISTICS OF PEOPLE WHO HAVE DIFFICULTY RELATING TO OTHERS

Relationships depend very much on circumstances. These are some of the characteristics which help to create difficult relationships.

- Their mistrust of others often shows in antagonism towards them.
- They may so fear being 'discovered' that they avoid close personal ties and only establish superficial relationships.
- Their fear of rejection and being unloved makes them fearful of reaching out to others.
- If they are strongly competitive this may get in the way, because they always have to be the winner.
- They believe in 'togetherness' as an end in itself, for their own needs, not for mutual benefit.
- They always want to be in control of what happens in a relationship.
- Their desire to be liked, and for intimacy, can be overwhelming.
- They are often so strongly self-sufficient, due to their high sense of self-preservation, that they give the impression of not needing other people.
- They can be possessive of the other person.
- They like to be the centre of attention, and to be listened to, but are often not good listeners.
- Underneath they often feel worthless, unimportant and alienated from others.
- They may be so passive that they don't take any responsibility in relationships.
- They may be so introverted, private and withdrawn that others can't get near them.
- They can be so extraverted and full of life that they tend to wear other people down.
- They may be so afraid to show affection to one person that they keep everybody at a distance.
- They may find that making decisions is difficult or impossible.
- They may seek out people all the time, and want others to be with them, because they may feel anxious if others are not around to help them.
- They may find it impossible to openly challenge someone.

- They consider the lowest rung of a hierarchy to be the best place for them, so that others take charge.
- When people do not respond with intimacy they often resort to punishing them.

Exercise 3.8
When you have worked through the characteristics listed above, spend time thinking through the following:

1 What influences in your life helped develop the way you think, feel and behave?
2 How comfortable are you overall with how you relate to people?
3 What do you consider you need to change?
4 What strategies could you use to encourage change?

LEARNING THE LANGUAGE OF LOVE

I will close this chapter with an extract from a book by Denis Waitley, *Seeds of Greatness*.

'Valentines are love letters with simple statements of affection. Love is one of the few experiences in life that we can best keep by giving it away. Love is the act of demonstrating value for, and looking for, the good in another person.

L   is for Listen. To love is to listen unconditionally to someone's values and needs without prejudice.

O   is for Overlook. To love is to overlook the flaws and the faults, in favour of looking for the good.

V   is for Voice. To love is to voice your approval of that person on a regular basis. There is no substitute for honest encouragement, positive 'strokes' and praise.

E   is for Effort. To love is to make a constant effort to spend the time, to make the sacrifice, to go the extra mile, and to show your interest.'

SUMMARY

Relationships are complex, and can never be taken for granted. A relationship with one person cannot be replicated with someone else. Behaviour that is acceptable between two people will be unacceptable between others.

Relationships are exciting and rewarding, but if we are to make them work we have to understand ourselves as well as other people. Understanding the basic principles of relationship-building is essential if we are to get on with people. We cannot be forced to relate well to people; we have to want to.

Understanding why we think, feel and behave the way we do helps us to avoid making mistakes with people. And when things do go wrong, knowing what makes us and other people tick helps us to put things right.

However, and this is important, we may get on with most people very well, but there are always some people with whom we will never get on. The chemistry does not work. Even the most relationship-skilled person cannot succeed every time. Knowing when to walk away and cut your losses is an essential element in self-preservation. To keep bashing your head on a stone wall is both painful and silly.

Seeing gradual change

If, having read through this chapter and worked through the exercises you find yourself thinking, feeling and behaving differently, even just a little, then you are putting into practice what you are reading.

Don't expect dramatic changes; life is not like that, neither are relationships. Take a lesson from nature. You may watch all day and not see a plant grow; but come back in a month and the growth will be obvious. Let your relationship-building skills be like that. Let growth and change happen naturally. Above all, take heart! If you don't get it right the first time, keep on until you do. As long as you live, and however old you may be, there is always more to learn about getting on with people.

> Let your relationships bring you great satisfaction and immense pleasure.

4

Developing Self-Knowledge

In this chapter we discuss self-knowledge, for without a degree of that we shall never make headway with developing the specific qualities essential for getting on with people.

Self-awareness is being aware of our physical, mental, emotional, moral, spiritual and social qualities which together make us unique individuals. They are all working together to help us towards our fullest potential.

It is doubtful if any of us truly *knows* who we are. Life is a constant discovery about parts of us that remain hidden from our conscious knowledge until we take active steps to become aware of them. Indeed many of us would rather others did not know our true self. Yet this, by itself, can put us under great pressure. Generally it is less stressful to be true than to be false.

UNDERSTANDING SELF-KNOWLEDGE

Learning to get on with people requires constant appraisal of who we are: our thoughts, feelings, behaviours, attitudes, motives and values. This is called self-knowledge.

Knowing who we are does not mean that we ever truly know ourselves, once and for all. Self-knowledge is not like learning to drive a car, where we take a test and walk away with proof that we have passed the test and can throw away our L-plates. Rather, it is a journey of discovery. As soon as we reach one goal, see one new vista, another stretches ahead of us, enticing us forward – ever forward.

> The road signposted 'self-knowledge' is full of excitement and challenge.

But unlike a journey, if we are to progress to the next vista we must incorporate the insights we have gained so far along the road.

Thus we are building up our self-knowledge bit by bit, stage by stage.

Much of what is contained in this book hinges on your ability to explore yourself. Some of the challenges we encounter are to do with being honest and open with ourselves, for our willingness to be open and honest will be reflected in our relationships.

There is no guarantee that increased self-knowledge will bring 'happiness' – a very transient feeling – however it will bring a certain sense of wholeness. When people are low on awareness they do not know themselves well. It is difficult to be open with themselves if they do not know who they are. If they are not self-aware they often behave in ways that they do not understand. They are strangers to themselves and they often do not understand why they behave in the way they do.

When we are very high on awareness, we may begin to wallow in ourselves and to lose contact with the world. When we are so self-occupied and introspective we may not pay attention to anything outside of ourselves. On the journey we may go through such a period but then move on to a more constructive level.

People who are aware know themselves well and are aware of, and comfortable with, themselves. They are not dark and unknown or brilliantly bright. They strive to be simply clear and open. Above all they strive to be appropriately open, honest and available.

Exercise 4.1   Assessing how aware you are of yourself

1 How well do you know what makes you tick?
2 How open are you with yourself? Or are you, even in secret, not frank with yourself? Answering this question might be the start of your journey of discovery.
3 How comfortable do you feel with yourself?
4 If you feel uncomfortable, can you track this feeling to its source? It may be a relationship from the past that is still haunting you.

IDENTIFYING WHAT SELF-KNOWLEDGE IS

1 To be aware of our own personality, qualities and continuing identity.
2 To strive to integrate our physical, mental, emotional, moral,

spiritual and social qualities so that together they work towards us achieving our fullest potential.

3 The capacity to understand and use our qualities, to focus attention, process information in accord with the self-concept.

4 Engaging in free and open exchange of information.

5 Engaging in behaviour that is public and freely available, but always appropriate.

6 Being aware that we have motives, feelings and behaviours which are perceived by others, of which we may not be fully aware, and communicating these by what we say, and how we say it, as well as by what we communicate non-verbally.

7 Being aware that we have things that are private and secret that we rarely disclose because we fear being hurt, rejected or judged.

8 Being aware that at the deeper level of the unconscious there are things that are so deeply hidden that we cannot normally access them, but that they influence who we are.

9 Understanding that there are early childhood memories and feelings, latent potentialities, and unrecognised conflicts and complexes which often come to trouble our dreams and create difficulties in our relationships.

Exercise 4.2   Assessing awareness of who you are

1 Answer by prefixing each pair of values with 'I am more . . . than I am . . .'

2 Place an X in one of the boxes between each pair of values.

3 When you have answered all the questions, connect all the Xs to give your profile.

4 When you have created your profile, ask someone who knows you very well to comment on how accurately you know yourself.

affectionate	☐	☐	☐	☐	☐	cold
arrogant	☐	☐	☐	☐	☐	modest
agreeable	☐	☐	☐	☐	☐	contradictory
boring	☐	☐	☐	☐	☐	interesting
compassionate	☐	☐	☐	☐	☐	severe
conventional	☐	☐	☐	☐	☐	modern
dominant	☐	☐	☐	☐	☐	passive
easy-going	☐	☐	☐	☐	☐	demanding
exacting	☐	☐	☐	☐	☐	tolerant
friendly	☐	☐	☐	☐	☐	aloof

hesitant	☐	☐	☐	☐	☐	adventurous
happy	☐	☐	☐	☐	☐	sad
hard	☐	☐	☐	☐	☐	sensitive
impulsive	☐	☐	☐	☐	☐	cautious
introvert	☐	☐	☐	☐	☐	extravert
insecure	☐	☐	☐	☐	☐	secure
industrious	☐	☐	☐	☐	☐	lazy
intellectual	☐	☐	☐	☐	☐	practical
inattentive	☐	☐	☐	☐	☐	attentive
imaginative	☐	☐	☐	☐	☐	dull
incompetent	☐	☐	☐	☐	☐	competent
lively	☐	☐	☐	☐	☐	quiet
light-hearted	☐	☐	☐	☐	☐	serious
moody	☐	☐	☐	☐	☐	stable
mature	☐	☐	☐	☐	☐	immature
mean	☐	☐	☐	☐	☐	generous
open	☐	☐	☐	☐	☐	secretive
pessimistic	☐	☐	☐	☐	☐	optimistic
patient	☐	☐	☐	☐	☐	impatient
rigid	☐	☐	☐	☐	☐	flexible
reliable	☐	☐	☐	☐	☐	unreliable
submissive	☐	☐	☐	☐	☐	assertive
self-confident	☐	☐	☐	☐	☐	unsure
shy	☐	☐	☐	☐	☐	sociable
tense	☐	☐	☐	☐	☐	relaxed
unattractive	☐	☐	☐	☐	☐	likeable
unresolved	☐	☐	☐	☐	☐	persistent
unaspiring	☐	☐	☐	☐	☐	ambitious

This is not a scientific questionnaire, but one that has arisen out of my work in groups. There is no right or wrong profile. Everybody is unique. Here are some pointers to how you might make use of the profile.

1 The scoring of most people swings from one side to the other – quite rightly so – and they arrive at a profile they feel represents them fairly accurately.
2 If you scored right down the middle, or nearly so, how honest were you being with yourself?
3 If your score is very markedly to one side only, consider how you might move towards a wider spread.

4 How many of these characteristics help you get along with people?

5 How many of these characteristics hinder you in getting along with people?

6 All of these characteristics affect how we relate to people.

7 Which characteristics could you work on to improve your relationships?

KEEPING RELATIONSHIPS GOING

Getting on with people means more than being able to establish relationships; it means keeping them healthy and alive. Finding new people to relate to is exciting, and many of us go through life making contact with people yet fail to maintain those relationships. Of course this is influenced by the other person.

Sometimes relationships which start out with great promise, and for a time are fulfilling and dynamic, go stale and fizzle out and die. There may be many reasons why this happens; it may be something to do with us, something within our personality that does not meet the other person's expectations and needs, or vice versa.

One of the aims of this book is to help you explore possible reasons why relationships work or don't work, and to suggest ways in which you might start to put things right. The following section will help you to examine some of the things that you can look at to ensure that you are doing all *you* can to keep the relationship alive and well.

WHAT YOU CAN DO TO KEEP RELATIONSHIPS ALIVE

1 Get on the other person's wavelength.

2 Listen, and respond in such a way that the other person knows you have heard.

3 Try to understand what the message means to the other person.

4 Wait for a response to what you have said.

5 Don't be afraid of or uncomfortable with silences.

6 Learn to read between the lines, but don't play the amateur psychologist.

7 Don't be always probing for hidden psychological meanings.

8 Try to understand the feelings of the other person. Remember, feelings are the cement that keeps the word-bricks together. Words are vehicles for feelings.

9 Try to get inside the other person's frame of reference. This means trying to see the world through the other person's eyes.

10 Demonstrate empathy.

11 Express support.

12 Learn to express your own feelings in a constructive way.

13 Learn to avoid making assumptions about what the other person means. Ask for clarification.

14 Don't make sexist or racist remarks or patronising comments about age.

15 Build each other up, without being patronising or condescending.

16 Learn to express caring in the way the other person appreciates.

17 Be committed to the relationship.

18 Don't talk about one person to another, unless what you say builds the other person up.

19 Don't attribute blame to the other person when you don't hit it off.

20 Learn to co-operate, not to compete for the time you have together.

21 Learn how best you can encourage the other person.

22 Work out how you can both get the most out of the relationship; this may mean learning to compromise.

23 Learn to respect the differences between you so that you both gain.

24 Learn to say what you want to say, yet with tact and discretion.

25 Demonstrate the language of love (as in Chapter 3).

26 Learn to be tolerant.

27 Learn to respect the other person's values, as much as yours are respected.

28 There is no such thing as the 'perfect relationship'. Don't waste precious time searching for it. It is a myth. Make the most of the relationships you have. Do all you can to make them work. Let every relationship enrich your life. Don't chase a fantasy.

29 Laugh and enjoy humour, but not at the expense of the other person. And don't use laughter as a cover-up to disclosing what you think or how you feel.

30 Learn that it's OK to say sorry. But being able to say sorry should not mean that you carry on doing something that creates tension in your relationship. The other person's goodwill might run out.

LEARNING TO BE OPEN-MINDED

In Chapter 3 we discussed a little of what it means to be open in relationships. This section develops that theme. However, before continuing it is necessary to draw attention to the fact that being open or closed is neither good nor bad. If in being open we are so transparent that we are naïve and taken in, then we might put ourselves into danger. We must always strive for balance, recognising when it is appropriate to be open, and when it would be more appropriate to be discreet. Knowing when it is appropriate is an essential quality of being an aware person.

Total openness with everyone is to be naïve and innocent. While there is a place for both of these characteristics, they have to be balanced with wordly wisdom. Although we speak of openness we must learn when, and to whom, we can be open and what is appropriate or inappropriate to reveal. On the other hand, to be secretive and closed does little to foster effective relationships. In reality, the people who are closed and secretive generally have little to be ashamed about. The skeletons in their cupboards, if they allow people to look in, are no worse than those in anyone else's, though to them they are.

Identifying what open-mindedness is

Open-mindedness refers to how flexible and responsive we are to examining new evidence about who we are. Open-mindedness is partially related to our ability to receive, evaluate and act on information from the outside on its own merits.

Internal pressures

Open-mindedness also relates to how we are able to free ourselves from *internal pressures* that would obscure or interfere with incoming information.

Examples of irrelevant internal pressures would be:

● habits
● beliefs

- perceptions
- motives
- power needs
- self-praise needs
- the need to allay anxiety.

External pressures
Examples of *external pressures* would be relying on reward or punishment from external authority, such as:

- parents
- peers
- other authority figures
- reference groups
- social, institutional and cultural norms.

Open-minded people are not influenced by high status.

IDENTIFYING LACK OF OPENNESS IN RELATIONSHIPS

Part of developing self-knowledge is being honest with yourself as to the reasons why you find it easy to be open with some people, and do not feel open with others. As you read through this section think how each of the 15 points applies to you, and in which relationships.

People who lack openness:

- Are often difficult to approach.
- Are often insensitive to others' needs and goals.
- Often resist other people's suggestions and ideas.
- Often expect too much of other people.
- Tend to be highly competitive.
- Often find it difficult to be objective, and frequently take comments personally.
- Are resistant to change.
- Are unwilling to understand from someone else's point of view.
- Are often resentful of outside suggestions.
- Often refuse offers of help.
- Find it difficult to co-operate.

- Are often unwilling to adjust to reality.
- Find it difficult to change their ways of doing things.
- Are frequently insensitive to the effects they have on others.
- Are generally difficult to approach.

LEARNING TO ENCOURAGE EACH OTHER

Encouraging each other is an important factor in keeping relationships on track. Encouragement communicates trust, respect and belief. Many psychologists contend that there are only two basic human emotions: love and fear.

- Encouragement communicates caring and movement towards others – love.
- Discouragement results in lowered self-esteem and alienation from others – fear.

Yet despite the intention to be encouraging, all too often we discourage people. An example is the manager or parent who 'lets things go' as long as they are going well, and who comments only when things go wrong. A crucial start to being a more encouraging person is to become more aware of, and to eliminate, discouraging messages.

What you can do to encourage people
Do
1 Value people as they are, not as their reputations indicate or as you hope they will be.
2 Believe people to be good and worthwhile and act towards them accordingly.
3 Have faith in the abilities of others. This enables you to win confidence while building the self-respect of the other person.
4 Show faith in people, and this will help them to believe in themselves.
5 Recognise honest effort as well as honest achievement.
6 Plan for success and assist in the development of skill.
7 Focus on strengths and assets rather than on mistakes.
8 Use people's interests in order to motivate learning and instruction.

Don't
1 Concentrate on errors and make frequent use (metaphorically) of the red pencil.

2 Think of relationships in terms of superiority/inferiority. Rather think of them in terms of equality and mutuality.
3 Practise one-upmanship by trying to discover other people who perform worse than you do, so that you can tell yourself how good you are.
4 Carry on making decisions and arriving at conclusions, with habits acquired in childhood and which are no longer appropriate as adults. Learn to confront outworn patterns of thinking and behaving.
5 Concentrate on weaknesses and ignore strengths.

Use specific words of encouragement

- *You do a good job of* . . . Try to encourage people when they do not expect it, or when they are not asking for it. A comment about something that may seem small and insignificant could have a significant positive impact.
- *You have improved in* . . . Encouragement assists growth and helps people improve. If you comment on any progress, there is less chance of discouragement and people will usually continue to try.
- *I like (enjoy) you, but I don't like what you do.* People frequently feel disliked after having made mistakes or after misbehaving. Rather, it is important to distinguish between the individual and his or her behaviour. In other words, you are saying: I love you just the same – unconditionally.
- *You can help me by* . . . To feel useful and helpful is important to everyone. Most people need only to be given an opportunity.
- *Let us try it together.* When we think that we have to do things perfectly we are often afraid to attempt something for fear of making mistakes or failing.
- *So you made a mistake; now, what can you learn from it?* Mistakes can teach us a great deal, especially if we do not feel embarrassed for trying.
- *You'd like me to think that you can't do it, but I think you can.* A person who tries and fails can be complimented for having the courage to try. Expectations should be consistent with ability and maturity.
- *Keep trying; don't give up.* This demonstrates faith in the other person's ability.
- *I am sure that you can straighten this out (solve this problem), but if you need any help, you know where you can find me.* Making yourself available but not taking over.

- *I understand how you feel – however, I'm sure you will be able to handle it.* Sympathy seldom helps because it does nothing to empower. Empathy and believing in the person's ability is positive and energising.

LEARNING THE SELF-HELP WAY OF WORTH AND CONFIDENCE

1 **Self-affirmation**. An appreciation of your strengths, motives, values and experiences.
2 **Self-determination**. Being able to take responsibility for your life without blaming others.
3 **Self-motivation**. Setting goals and taking the action necessary to reach those goals by integrating your emotions and intellect with your body.
4 **Empathy**. Developing increased empathic regard for others is self-enhancing.

> Many people's feelings of inadequacy can be overcome by substituting negative self-talk with positive affirmation. Encouragement can assist us to rediscover our values and joys, to identify strengths instead of dwelling on mistakes, to challenge and change old patterns, and to have the courage to be imperfect!

CASE STUDY

Zoe is encouraged

In the June 1999 issue of *Reader's Digest* (p. 87) is the story of Zoe Kiplowitz. She recounts how, as a sufferer of multiple sclerosis, she ran in her first New York marathon. It took her 19 hours and 57 minutes to complete the course.

Five years later she met her marathon heroine, Grete Waitz. They formed a firm friendship. Grete insisted on being at the finishing line for Zoe's sixth marathon. 'I'll be there for you, no matter how long it takes,' Grete assured Zoe. It took her 28 hours to cross the finishing line. Because the medal box had been stolen, Grete commandeered her husband's medal of the day before, and was there to hang it around Zoe's neck when she broke through the tape. Grete has been there for Zoe at the finishing line of every marathon since.

SUMMARY

Knowing one's self is a bit like sailing into the horizon; as soon as you reach it, it stretches tantalisingly away from you. The journey of self-knowledge, or self-awareness, never ends, or should never end. Like knowledge, there is more to learn than we have ever learnt. When we say we know all there is to know about ourselves, we start to die.

The aim of self-knowledge is not happiness; it is wholeness. It is the development of mind, body and spirit; of thoughts, feelings, behaviour and spirituality. Too much concentration on one could be at the expense of the others, and of wholeness. So far as this book is concerned, self-knowledge has as its purpose – getting on with people. However, many people can't get along with themselves, let alone form relationships with others. Part of the excitement of travelling the pathway of self-knowledge is discovering more about ourselves. Some of what we discover we might not like, but whatever lies hidden is an essential part of ourselves. It has its origins somewhere, and it has grown within us and influences us in every aspect of our life. So don't despise what you discover. Rejoice that you know a bit more about yourself.

How self-knowledge helps
Self-knowledge will help you to look at the good and the not so good; the things you like about yourself and those that you detest. Yet good can come from the things you discover you would rather not admit to.

As an example I have had a stammer since childhood, and at times I've wished it would disappear. But now, in my 70s, it is still with me. I have had three successful careers; have engaged in public speaking; have sung in competitions and over the past 30 years have written extensively. I maintain that I am a writer *because* I have a stammer. Some of the difficulties I have with communication have inspired me to become a wordsmith.

How about you? Turn to good use your journey of self-discovery, for yourself and for others.

Above all, let your self-knowledge be an aid to how you get on with people.

5

Developing Relationship Qualities

In Chapter 4 we discussed self-knowledge as an essential ingredient in relationships. Here we discuss certain qualities crucial to relationships.

Five words tell us what to avoid in getting on with people:
- distance
- meddling
- commanding
- preaching
- imposing.

When these are replaced with:
- affection
- warmth
- empathy
- genuineness
- and regard

then we have a recipe for relationship success.

QUALITY 1 – UNDERSTANDING THE NEED FOR AFFECTION

Affection is the emotional fertiliser that keeps relationships flourishing and healthy, yet for many people affection is the one quality that is so difficult to express. Studies of children in institutions revealed harrowing evidence that when deprived of stimulation, touch, cuddles, or just seeing other children or adults, the child would be liable to grow up with an inability to receive affection yet would constantly crave it.

There are two special characteristics of affection which it is helpful to consider – touch and warmth. We shall consider touch later, as a means of communication, and warmth later in this chapter as one of the relationship qualities.

Identifying the need for affection in relationships
- Has to do with being *warm* or *cold* in relationships.
- It is giving and receiving friendship.
- Some people want close relationships, others want distant relationships.
- Some want close relationships with one person, others with many people.

Exercise 5.1   Assessing affection in your relationships
1 In which relationships are you able to express the affection you want to?
2 In which relationships are you unable to express the affection you want to?
3 What are your feelings when your affection is rejected?

QUALITY 2 – UNDERSTANDING THE NEED FOR WARMTH

Warmth may be non-possessive or possessive. **Non-possessive warmth** is genuine, and springs from an attitude of friendliness towards others. It makes us feel comfortable because it liberates, and is non-demanding. It melts the coldness and hardness within people's hearts.

On the other hand **possessive warmth** is false, and makes us feel uncomfortable and wary, because it is perceived as non-genuine. It is more for the needs of the giver than for the receiver. It is smothering and cloying, and robs us of energy.

Identifying how we convey warmth
Body language
- posture
- proximity
- personal space
- facial expressions
- eye contact.

Words and the way we speak
- words that convey warmth and feeling, like using a person's name rather than just 'hello'

- tone of voice
- delivery
- rate of speech
- the use of non-words ('paralinguistics').

All the indicators of warmth — the non-verbal parts of speech and body language – must be in agreement with the words used. Any discrepancy between the words and how we deliver them will create confusion. Other people will not know how to respond.

Things you can do to demonstrate warmth
1 Show genuine concern.
2 Show appreciation.
3 Think of others as people of worth.
4 Accept criticism without taking umbrage.
5 Help people to feel safe with you by not criticising or condemning.
6 Help people to be themselves.
7 Make it OK for people to talk about anything they want to.
8 Trust people to know what is right and wrong *for themselves*. To think that you know best is patronising and demeaning.
9 Never knowingly hurt other people.

QUALITY 3 – UNDERSTANDING THE NEED FOR EMPATHY

Empathy is a word we hear a great deal, and however essential it is in getting on with people it is a transient quality which sometimes eludes us. However experienced we are in the business of relationships, there are times when our empathy will desert us; when we cannot get on the other person's wavelength.

As a counsellor, empathy is central to my work, but there are times when I know, and the client knows, that my empathy has slipped. If they are honest, all counsellors will say the same thing. So take heart! If you are just starting out on this relationship journey, there will be times when empathy, and all the other qualities talked about in this book, will seem to have deserted you. All I can say is: keep going. Keep trying. Determine that you will learn from the mistakes of yesterday, and so enhance the way you relate to people today and all the days ahead.

Defining what empathy is

- Empathy is the ability which we develop to step into the inner world of another person and to step out of it again. At all times we remain ourselves.
- It is trying to understand the thoughts, feelings, behaviours and personal meanings from the other's frame of reference. To see the world through the other person's eyes.
- It is the ability to imagine yourself in another's place and understand the other's feelings, desires, ideas and actions.
- It is to feel 'with' the other person.
- Empathy is enabling and empowering.
- Empathy is never assuming you know what the other person means.

Identifying what empathy is not

- It is not becoming the other person. Empathy works within the framework of 'as if' I were that other person, how would I feel?
- It is not a state that one reaches; not a qualification that one is awarded. It means getting – and staying – 'alongside' the other person.
- It is not sympathy, which is to feel 'like' the other person feels.
- It is not pity, which is to feel 'for' the other person. Both sympathy and pity do not empower the other person. They rob the person of emotional energy.

Things you can do to demonstrate empathy

1 Respond in such a way that the other person feels that you are trying to understand.
2 Make sure that your body language agrees with what you say.
3 Learn as much as you can about what makes you and the other person tick.
4 Try to understand how the other person sees things.
5 Show your understanding in as many different ways as possible.
6 Learn to listen to surface and deeper facts and feelings, as well as paying attention to body language.
7 Learn how to put the other person's feelings into words.
8 Learn to pick up on and reflect the other person's moods.
9 Learn to say things that reflect the other's feelings.

CASE STUDY

The singer who missed her cue

I was at a concert in the Royal Festival Hall. The singer, followed by her piano accompanist, looked confident and radiant. The pianist played the introduction to a ballad. The singer started, then stopped. She had hit the wrong starting note. She tried again and the same thing happened. She succeeded at the third attempt.

I would guess that the whole audience felt as I did, acutely embarrassed for the singer and her accompanist. At the same time there was a huge feeling of willing the singer to continue. The applause she received at the end of her recital was long and loud.

QUALITY 4 – UNDERSTANDING THE NEED TO BE GENUINE

Genuineness is the degree to which we are freely and deeply ourselves, without sham or pretence. Genuineness is the basis of open communication. It is being honest with, and about, ourselves, and communicating our feelings that mean something to the other person. It is the degree to which we are able to relate to people in a sincere and non-defensive manner.

Genuineness is also referred to as authenticity, congruence and truth. It is the precondition for empathy and unconditional regard. It is an aim; it is not a state, or a condition.

Identifying the place of genuineness in relationships

Effective relationships depend wholly on the degree to which we are integrated and genuine. Being genuine encourages healthy self-disclosure. Appropriate disclosure enhances genuineness. Genuineness does not *compel* others to disclose, either about events, situations, or feeling aroused within the relationship.

Things you can do to demonstrate genuineness

1 Strive for congruence between what you feel and what you say.
2 In your relationships be totally yourself. Don't hide behind facades.
3 Try to avoid hiding from yourself what you feel about the other person.
4 Try not to avoid anything that is important for your relationship.
5 Do all you can to foster a relationship of trust.
6 Try to demonstrate that your relationship is secure.

7 Relate to the other person with genuine and appropriate concern.

QUALITY 5 – UNDERSTANDING THE NEED FOR REGARD

Conditional regard implies enforced control and compliance, with behaviour dictated by someone else. **Unconditional regard** implies respect for the other person's uniqueness. Unconditional regard is one of the central qualities of getting on with people. It is a non-possessive acceptance of the other person, by which we communicate a deep and genuine caring, not filtered through our own feelings, thoughts and behaviours. Trying to offer unconditional regard to someone if we have not first experienced it is difficult. We cannot offer it if our self-esteem is at rock-bottom.

Unconditional regard is respect in action. It dissolves feelings of hatred, bitterness and resentment. It does not attach qualifying clauses: 'I will love you only if . . .'

Things you can do to demonstrate regard
1 Always try to respond with warmth and interest.
2 Try not to let a change in the person's feelings govern how you feel towards him or her.
3 Encourage other people to express whatever feelings they want, without taking offence.
4 Try to be appreciative of the other person.

SUMMARY OF THE FIVE RELATIONSHIP QUALITIES
- When affection, warmth, empathy, genuineness and unconditional regard are present, and appropriately expressed, a positive climate is created in which a relationship can flourish.
- The central qualities depend on the active demonstration of acceptance.
- When we demonstrate the central qualities, we encourage wholeness.
- We cannot reject someone and show unconditional regard at the same time.
- The pursuit of power, authority, or control and dominance over others destroys relationships and is the opposite of unconditional regard.

SUMMARY

In this chapter we have explored five relationship qualities. While all of these are essential, it is highly doubtful if any one person possesses all of them in all their fullness. But that does not prevent us from developing them.

Possessing these qualities to a lesser or greater degree does not mean that we turn them on like a tap. It does not mean that we decide to use, for example, empathy to suit a particular situation, for that would be manipulative. Rather, we absorb the qualities into our personality, so that they are gradually integrated, a bit like the ingredients in a cake. When we take a slice of cake we may be aware of, for example, bits of chocolate, fruit, peel, and so on, but other ingredients, like the sugar and the butter, and eggs are so incorporated throughout the cake that their individuality cannot be distinguished, but their influence is felt. So it is with relationship qualities.

Understanding how these qualities keep relationships healthy is an incentive for doing all we can to develop and demonstrate them. You may not feel confident about putting them all into practice, but select one and work on that, and you will find that not only will you gain confidence in relating to people, you will discover that people start to feel more comfortable with you. You have put relationship qualities to work.

Affection

Affection might be difficult to define, but we know when someone is being affectionate towards us. Of equal importance, we know when someone is cold towards us and has withdrawn affection. Being able to show people affection, appropriately, hinges on a secure self-esteem. Being able to receive affection, likewise, is related to a healthy self-esteem, a feeling that we are worthy of such affection.

Warmth

The second of the central qualities is warmth. What is important to draw from this lesson is that there is a pretend warmth and a genuine warmth. The false, or conditional, warmth is sugary, cloying, demanding and manipulative; it does nothing to promote equality in relationships. By contrast genuine warmth promotes growth of the highest order.

Empathy
We hear much about empathy, yet quite simply it is seeing, hearing and feeling as if we were that other person, yet always remaining ourselves.

Genuineness
Genuineness may be difficult to analyse, yet we have that gut reaction when we meet someone who is genuine. Genuineness is not packeted like the latest breakfast cereal; it springs from wells deep within, and comes out pure and unadulterated.

Unconditional regard
Unconditional regard is supreme respect. Because it is unconditional, as with affection, warmth, empathy and genuineness, it promotes growth. When our regard is conditional we imply that certain negative consequences will follow. Unconditional regard in relationships is not a soft option. It demands maturity and a deep sense of purpose.

When affection, warmth, empathy, genuineness and regard are present, the relationship will have five firm foundations to build on.

6

Developing Relationship Principles

In Chapter 5 we explored the relationship qualities of affection, empathy, warmth, genuineness and regard. The seven relationship principles of this chapter build on those qualities. The seven principles discussed here are:

- respecting individuality
- handling feelings
- being involved
- allowing choice
- acceptance
- not passing judgement
- and keeping confidences.

When these qualities and principles are present, and appropriately expressed, a climate is created in which a relationship will be encouraged to grow.

As you study these seven principles, please remember that they are not something fanciful, and only for superpeople. They are for everybody who wants to get on with people. They are for you.

PRINCIPLE 1 – LEARNING TO RESPECT INDIVIDUALITY

Respecting individuality means recognising and respecting every person's uniqueness. Most people like to think of themselves as unique, and detest being treated as one of the crowd, nothing more than a number on a list. We cannot have a relationship with an anonymous number. We do not relate to any old human being but to this specific human being – just as he or she is.

If someone does not respect our unique self, we feel put down, dismissed and worthless. But relating to the unique person in this way may not come easily. It is something most of us have to learn. Since we are all uniquely different, our needs are also equally different.

Effective relationships, therefore, must seek to meet each other's needs. We each use our abilities and resources to work together for the mutual benefit of each other and the relationship.

We must always remember that each partner in a relationship has physical, intellectual, emotional, social, spiritual, conscious and unconscious needs.

Conveying your respect for a person's individuality

- Listen and respond accurately to what the other person is saying.
- Respond with empathy, without dropping into platitudes.
- Try to keep perspective and in touch with reality.
- Demonstrate flexibility.
- Demonstrate thoughtfulness in details.
- Keep confidences.
- Show care and consideration over details.
- Do what gives pleasure and avoid what brings displeasure.
- Engage in a partnership, not in combat.

Becoming an effective relationship builder

Some people have a natural ability for DIY, and can knock up a wall never having had proper training. Some are very skilled at it; others never attempt it. We often talk of 'relationship-building', and this is very much what relationships are – building and hard work. Some people are fortunate enough to have acquired relationship skills early in life. For many of us, however, building relationships is hard work.

What you can do to become an effective relationship builder:

- Go for counselling.
- Take a course in interpersonal training or group work.
- Recognise and deal with your biases and prejudices.
- Acquire knowledge of human behaviour.

PRINCIPLE 2 – LEARNING TO HANDLE FEELINGS

We all have the right to our own feelings. We should neither discourage nor condemn feelings. Many of us experience discomfort when we have certain feelings, yet feelings are neither good nor bad; they become positive or negative when we act on them. They take on positive and negative overtones as we attach values to them. For example, anger is not bad; it becomes 'bad' when it influences our behaviour to act aggressively towards other people.

Expressing our feelings, particularly negative ones, can help to relieve pressure and tension and enable us to take positive, constructive action. Being in a relationship in which feelings are freely expressed leads to clearer understanding of each other. A climate in which feelings are expressed, and not condemned, helps both people to appreciate the other's strengths and weaknesses. Feelings shared provide emotional support and bring people closer.

Very often relationships break down because feelings are kept under lock and key, because we consider it wrong to have them and even worse to express them. If you do take time to listen, before the feelings reach flash point, you may prevent a destructive outburst as feelings are transmitted into behaviour.

Exploring feeling and thinking

We communicate much more than words or ideas. Words are vehicles for feelings. Both words and feelings must be listened to. We listen on three levels:

1 Thinking about the words and their underlying meanings.
2 Hearing the underlying feelings.
3 Hearing the intentions the words carry.

A barrier to expressing feelings is not being able to find the right word. We can help ourselves and other people get in touch with feelings by choosing appropriate words to identify them. The other side of this is that the more we work with feeling words, the more extensive our feelings vocabulary becomes.

What you can do to help someone express feelings

- Be comfortably relaxed.
- Be prepared mentally and emotionally.
- Listen attentively and purposefully.
- Be sensitively encouraging.
- Stay in tandem with the person; don't rush ahead; don't lag behind.
- Don't offer empty reassurances, or platitudes or clichés. They can sound patronising and uncaring.
- Try not to be afraid of hearing feelings, whether positive or negative.

- Be assured, helping people to express their negative feelings will rarely result in unacceptable behaviour. Hearing someone's anger, for example, will act like lifting the valve of a pressure cooker before it bursts.

Exercise 6.1   Working with your feelings
Picture yourself in a situation when you felt:

1 anger	7 hate
2 sadness	8 confusion
3 joy	9 boredom
4 fear	10 inferiority
5 embarrassment	11 loneliness
6 guilt	12 rejection

In each situation, try to become aware of what is happening in your mind, your body and your emotions. When you are aware of something happening in your body, mind or emotions, try to stay with it and not shrug it off. The more you allow your feelings to speak to you, the more self-understanding you will gain and the more accurate will be your understanding of other people's feelings.

Exercise 6.2   Exploring your feelings
This exercise follows on from the one above.

1 Take one of the words you worked with, perhaps one that caused you the most pain.
2 Write an imaginary letter to a close friend. Tell him or her about the incident. Make it a factual one, without any feelings in it.
3 Rewrite your letter, and for every fact you identify include one or more feelings you associate with the fact.
4 What is the difference between the two letters?

PRINCIPLE 3 – LEARNING TO GET INVOLVED

Emotional involvement in relationships is vital. Involvement means commitment. Involvement may be measured along a dimension:

No emotional involvement means **separation**	Engaged involvement means **contact**	Over-involvement means **engulfment**
↑	↑	↑

Dimension of involvement

Discussion of the model

A relationship in which there is no emotional involvement will be distant and cold. Indeed, it could be argued that if there is no emotional involvement there is no relationship, or it is casual and without much meaning. It is as if there is a barrier causing separation. In addition to coldness, there is a feeling of fear that any emotional involvement will result in loss of self-identity.

At the other end of the dimension is engulfment. That is where either one or both people in the relationship have become swamped, engulfed by the other person, so that they cannot identify themselves as separate people. That is scary. And it is that possibility that frightens many people off from ever developing relationships except on a casual basis. The characteristics of engulfment, in addition to not being able to separate from the other person or the relationship, are a feeling of either being possessed by the other person, or of possessing the other person, and of dominance. There is an overwhelming feeling of being suffocated, not necessarily by the other person but by the relationship itself. Any attempt to separate causes acute anxiety.

The ideal lies more towards 'engaged' involvement. The term engaged is drawn from an analogy of the gears of a car. Until the gears are engaged, the car will go nowhere.

Identifying the components of engaged involvement

1 **Sensitivity**. Listening to feelings, and observing verbal and non-verbal cues.
2 **Understanding**. What do the feelings mean to *this* person?

- **Get** into the person's frame of reference.
- **See** it through his/her eyes.
- **Hear** it through his/her ears.
- **Feel** it through his/her experience.
- **Increase** your understanding by talking to someone who really listens to you.

3 **Response**. Your response conveys your understanding. Sometimes the responses are verbalised; sometimes they need never be spoken.

PRINCIPLE 4 – LEARNING TO ALLOW CHOICE

A relationship in which there is no choice is not a relationship of equals. It does not respect the other person's uniqueness. Where there is no choice, one person in the relationship dominates the other, and this inequality breeds resentment and the relationship will fracture. In psychological terminology, choice is self-determination, or self-direction.

Self-determination is where we allow personal beliefs and values to determine our behaviour, rather than group pressures, or doing what society expects of us – and society includes all of us. Allowing the other person the right to make choices indicates a relationship of equality and maturity.

The basic right to freedom to choose your direction may clash with the values, beliefs, wishes and interests of other people, and the relationship may suffer. However, we all have the responsibility to live our life and achieve life's goals as we perceive them. One of the difficulties we might experience, particularly in close relationships, is that the chosen direction might mean the end of the relationship.

This is taking a serious and dramatic view of the principle of choice, but most of the time it never reaches such finality.

Identifying conflicts in allowing choice

One of the dilemmas you may have to face is: is the person's chosen direction potentially self-destructive? What if self-determination is potentially destructive to others?

Freedom is not licence. It is influenced by: the rights of others; the capacity to make informed decisions; civil and criminal constraints and a person's own morals. When we violate our own moral law, we do spiritual harm to ourselves. If there is a possibility of danger to self or others, it is questionable if we are being constructive if we do not challenge the decision. But in the end it is the person's choice, even though we may not agree with it.

Also, for every individual right of choice, there are accompanying duties and responsibilities in our relationship with others. When you believe in, and put into practice, the concept of self-determination, it does not mean that you are indifferent to what people do. Neither does it mean that you have to approve; you accept their right.

CASE STUDY

Jill learns to let go

Jill and her husband, David, were staunch members of the local evangelical church. They brought up their two daughters to be God-fearing, and to attend church. Both girls were very involved with all the youth activities at the church. Sarah, the elder daughter, was accepted to train for the ministry, and there were great expectations that Babs would follow in her sister's footsteps. At university Babs told her parents she was opting out and was going to live in a commune with a group of New Age people. They were horrified. Wise grandmother said: 'Give her your blessing. Let her travel her own journey.' They did, and Babs was very happy. Three years later she returned to university and went on to do social work.

By letting go, Jill kept her daughter.

PRINCIPLE 5 – LEARNING TO ACCEPT

Inherent in the idea of acceptance is that we do not judge people by some set of rules or standards. Acceptance is a special kind of loving which moves out towards people as they are – warts and all. Accepting someone means maintaining the person's dignity and personal worth. We acknowledge the person's strengths and weaknesses, favourable and unfavourable qualities, positive and negative attitudes, constructive and destructive wishes, thoughts, feelings and behaviours. It means that we do not wish or pressure to change the person to be someone else, someone we would wish him or her to become (often to become more like us!). Acceptance means that we do not wish to control, criticise or condemn (although we might not always live up to that standard). When we accept someone, we do not attach 'if' clauses; eg 'I will love you if . . .'

When we accept people just as they are, they accept us just as we are, with our strengths and weaknesses, with our successes and failures. But more than that: if we find it difficult to accept ourselves just as we are, we will find it difficult to accept other people just as they are.

Aspects of acceptance

The degree to which we accept other people is dependent on the degree of our own self-awareness. Only if we are well established psychologically are we able to relate to people in such a way that they can mobilise their feelings and energies towards growth and fulfilment. That is why getting on with people is enhanced by developing our self-knowledge.

We do not feel accepted unless the very worst in us is accepted too. We never feel accepted when judgement is passed on us. If we feel we have to be 'good' to be accepted, then that is not true acceptance.

Acceptance is not an all-or-nothing phenomenon, like perfect sight or total blindness. Rather, every one of us has a certain degree of acceptance, which may vary from day to day or from person to person. None of us has, or is expected to have, perfect acceptance, for that would require a godlike wisdom and an immunity from human frailties.

Acceptance is other-centred, directed to the needs of the other person, rather than to our own needs. Acceptance recognises the person's potential, and encourages the promotion of personal growth.

Identifying obstacles to acceptance

- Lack of knowledge of human behaviour.
- Being unwilling to explore blockages. For example, conscious hidden agendas, or unconscious unresolved conflicts, blind spots.
- Attributing one's own feelings to the other person.
- Allowing biases and prejudices, values, beliefs to get in the way.
- Jumping into offering unfounded reassurances, thereby putting an end to discussion.

- Being unwilling to explore issues which cause feelings of discomfort.
- Not being able to separate acceptance from approval of what someone does.
- Not being able to respect the other person as an individual of worth.

CASE STUDY

Danny shows his prejudice

Danny was a trainee social worker and coming to me for supervision. One of his placements was in a mental illness unit. One of the clients allocated to him was Bernard. As we discussed the allocation, he said: 'I can't work with him, he's gay. Homosexuality is a sin.' He then went on to expound what 'the Bible says about homosexuality.' 'And what does Jesus say about sinners?' I asked. 'Did he turn them away, any more than he turned the lepers away? Can we choose whom we want to accept or reject?'

Danny did work with Bernard (who was attending the unit for depression) and learnt that acceptance does not necessarily mean approval of the behaviour but of the person.

PRINCIPLE 6 – LEARNING NOT TO PASS JUDGEMENTS

Judgement is to do with law, blame, guilt or innocence, and punishment. If relationships are to work we must learn to suspend our judgements and standards and not to impose them on others. Judgementalism is critical, and condemns others because of their conduct or supposed false beliefs, wrong motives, or faulty character.

The result of judgementalism is that it dims, divides and fragments relationships. Judgementalism seeks to elevate one person above another. Within it are the characteristics of self-exaltation, self-promotion and the determination to be first on every occasion. We cannot relate to people effectively while we are judging and condemning them. When we pass judgement upon others, if we examine ourselves, we will find that the very thing on which we pass judgement is also present within ourselves in one degree or another.

Judgementalism can often be detected by such words as 'should,' 'ought,' 'must,' 'don't,' and by such phrases as 'in my opinion,' 'I think . . .' 'this is what you should do.'

Judgementalism is often associated with authority, control, hierarchy, rules and regulations that impose standards of behaviour. Judgementalism is the opposite of acceptance. Judgementalism paralyses. Acceptance affirms and encourages change.

What you can do to avoid being judgemental

- Recognise and carefully scrutinise your own values and standards.
- Try to see the world through the other person's eyes.
- Try to avoid jumping to conclusions, or making assumptions.
- Do not say, 'I know how you feel.'
- Do not compare one person to someone else.
- Do not become over-involved.
- Be receptive and accepting.
- Concentrate on the other person's feelings, not on the facts.
- Be interested in the whole person.
- Demonstrate sincere respect for the other as a person of worth.
- Facilitate, do not play the role of the psychoanalyst.
- Try to understand from the person's frame of reference.
- Get into the person's inner world.
- Don't rush to answer; be aware of your own values.
- Hear then respond to the expressed and implied feelings.
- Accept that people know more about themselves than you do.

Exercise 6.3   Identifying your feelings about being judged
Recall a situation in which you felt you were being judged.

1 How did you feel?
2 What did you want to do?
3 What feelings are you still left with?

PRINCIPLE 7 – LEARNING TO KEEP CONFIDENCES

This chapter ends with an outline of what **confidentiality** means. The more we become involved in relationships, the more aware we must be of the difficulties of keeping confidences.

Confidentiality has ethical overtones as well as an essential element in maintaining relationships. Confidentiality, at first glance, is deceptively simple. It means not disclosing secret details about another person which have been disclosed to us. Ensuring confidentiality is an obligation; breaching confidentiality is a breaking of trust and a misuse of a relationship.

Keeping confidences is more than being tight-lipped; it is being so aware of the other person and his or her needs that you will not talk about anything that would cause embarrassment, or bring shame or disgrace, or put that person in a bad light. It also means not passing on any information that has come to you directly or indirectly, even though the person has not said, 'Don't tell anybody.'

It means not gossiping or telling tales. Gossip, like rumour, tends to be like Chinese whispers, where the original message becomes distorted beyond recognition. People often gossip whether they do or do not believe the facts. The more the particular issue is repeated, the more people tend to believe it.

Exercise 6.4 Can you keep confidences?

If you do pass on a confidence, ask yourself why you did it. What were your motives? Ask yourself:

1 Did I want to gain prestige, because I have information no one else has?
2 Did I want to seem important and impress?
3 Did I want to develop a relationship with the person I disclosed to?
4 Do I like gossiping?
5 Does integrity mean less to me than passing something on?
6 Does the relationship now mean less to me than previously?
7 How far am I unable to distinguish what should be kept confidential from what is general knowledge?
8 If being indiscreet is your weakness, how can you start to change that?

CASE STUDY

Mary is concerned for Jane

Jane whispered to Mary over the garden fence that she had to go to the hospital for a cervical smear check up. 'They're not happy with it.' That was all. She did not say not to tell anybody.

Mary met Dorcas, who knew Jane, and told her. 'You won't say anything, will you, unless she does?' said Mary.

Dorcas has very strict views about keeping confidences, and when she next met Jane she asked in a casual way, 'How are you today?' and as Jane did not tell her, Dorcas kept the knowledge to herself. It was Jane's prerogative to tell her, if she wished. Later, when Jane had been to the specialist and the result was negative, then she told Dorcas.

Did Mary break a confidence?

SUMMARY

This chapter introduced seven fundamental relationship principles. When we relate to the uniqueness in people, rather than lump them together, we are relating to them with respect. When we don't listen to people's feelings, we do them an injustice. Hearing feelings may not come easily to everyone, that is why several feelings exercises were included.

Relationships mean involvement. What we should be aiming for is engagement, like engaging car gears, without which there would be no progress.

It may be easy to talk about giving people choice (self-determination) and how it is everybody's right to choose what is right for them, not for us. Yet someone else's self-determination may be our slavery. Self-determination borders on anarchy when the rights of others are ignored. Rights and duties exist side by side. You cannot have one without the other.

Working with the principles

Acceptance, a cornerstone in effective relationships according to Carl Rogers (originator of the person-centred approach to counselling), is a special kind of loving. It is akin to the love shown by a mother who, though seeing the horrid deformity of her child, discerns the child's soul and makes contact with the spirit, rather than with the outward appearance. If that sounds poetic, so be it. That is my understanding of acceptance. We accept people for who they are, not for what we would like them to be.

The principle of not passing judgement, for some of us (and I speak personally) is probably the most elusive of all the seven qualities. It is very easy to put ourselves in the roles of judge and jury. Unfortunately, the rules by which we judge people are usually known only to us; they are the standards by which we control our lives. Judgementalism is iniquitous, yet it pervades almost every relationship. Unless we take it by the scruff of the neck and control it, it will ruin any relationship.

The final principle of getting on with people – keeping confiddences – is more difficult than it seems on the surface. Without a strict code of not talking to one person about another, relationships would be in chaos. One aspect of confidentiality is not complaining to one person about someone else. It also means when someone else relates something to you about a third person, do not disclose what you already know unless it is common knowledge. Even then, be careful that you are not engaging in gossip.

> None of these seven principles is absolute. We should never say 'I have arrived,' but rather, 'I am travelling.'

7

Exploring Risk-Taking and Trust in Relationships

Getting involved with other people means we have to take risks. There is the risk that we might not be understood; that we might make a mess of the relationship; that we might be taken for a ride; that our overtures might be rejected. Yet the alternative to moving out towards people is that we remain isolated and alone. If we are content to be alone, that's fine, but if we want a relationship we have to take the risk of getting involved.

Risk-taking cannot be considered without also looking at trust. Trust is the foundation stone of relationships. Trust develops gradually and requires consistent and concentrated effort to maintain it.

IDENTIFYING TRUST LEVELS

Characteristics of people with high trust levels
They:

- accept other people's values and attitudes
- believe in equality
- try to help solve problems
- try to co-operate with people
- try to reach agreed decisions
- believe in freedom of expression
- try to be spontaneous and encourage spontaneity
- rate themselves as being highly dependable
- rate themselves as being highly genuine people
- strive to be open in their communication
- believe people recognise them as being competent
- try to relate with warmth and empathy
- try to demonstrate respect of others
- believe in holding themselves accountable

- try to support others
- try to treat others with regard
- try to understand other people's thoughts, feelings and behaviours
- are willing to take risks in relating to people.

Characteristics of people with low trust levels
They:

- always want to 'play it safe'
- communicate in a closed rather than open way
- are often cold and rejecting, and difficult to get to know
- are concerned with hierarchy and status
- have a strong need to be in control
- display feelings of superiority
- are often highly competitive
- are often openly hostile
- often display inconsistent standards and behaviour
- generally lack respect for others
- are generally not consistently reputable
- are often suspicious of other people's motives
- are generally unwilling to give credit
- are unwilling to take risks.

> When trust is destroyed, hurt and anger and a fear of ever trusting again develop. Effective relationships hinge on developing a trusting climate.

WHAT YOU CAN DO TO BUILD TRUST
1 Accept the feelings of others.
2 Be consistent.
3 Be present and involved.
4 Work for straightforward communication.
5 Develop effective eye contact.
6 Strive for empathic listening.
7 Express feelings.

8 Give and receive feedback.
9 Initiate contact.
10 Initiate communication.
11 Respect trusting behaviour in others.
12 Use 'I' talk, rather than 'one' or 'you'.
13 Use affirming language and behaviour.

Behaviours of trusting/open people
They:

- are able to be themselves and do not hide behind roles
- respond to current feelings and perceptions
- focus on relationships
- are spontaneous
- like sharing themselves with others
- respond to the uniqueness of others
- are concerned for their self-development and the development of others
- are not afraid to follow hunches and gut reactions
- focus more on positive than negative behaviours
- focus on the 'here and now', the real, rather than on what might be
- focus on strengths
- strive for agreement between their verbal and non-verbal communication.

> When trust levels are high, people are more open, more self-determining, more personal and more interdependent.

EXPLORING SELF-DISCLOSURE AND TRUST

Self-disclosure is the process by which we let ourselves be known to others. Sometimes we make a conscious decision to disclose something to another person. But equally, we are disclosing something about ourselves all the time, by our body language, which is mainly at an unconscious level. This section concentrates on conscious, verbal disclosure of our thoughts and feelings.

Clear verbal and non-verbal disclosures increase the chance of accurate reception without the need for complicated decoding. *Appropriate* disclosure is critical in relationships. It enhances them, keeps them alive and helps to avoid alienation. One person's low disclosure is likely to block another person's willingness to disclose. When we are genuine, in touch with our own inner empathy, we are also in touch with what we are experiencing and send authentic messages, rather than messages which conflict and confuse.

Disclosure involves both negative and positive aspects of self. Not everyone finds it easy to disclose positive aspects of themselves, possibly due to low self-esteem.

Suggested guidelines for disclosing something

1 Disclosing means that we have to anticipate:
   - our own feelings
   - the other person's reactions
   - the possible effect on the relationship.
2 We may hinder people's genuine self-disclosure by:
   - secrecy, which leads to a high degree of information control
   - colluding with them; fantasy and reality become confused
   - faking disclosures; prevents the other person from making genuine disclosures.
3 Questions about the appropriateness of disclosure:
   - how much?
   - what area and how many areas?
   - how intimate?
   - to whom?
   - in what context?
   - why am I doing it?

One of the risks of disclosure is that it might backfire. The last question above asks 'Why am I doing it?' While disclosing something about yourself certainly might help to deepen the relationship, if the motive is suspect then it could harm the relationship. Some people disclose something to another person too soon in the relationship, and this has the effect of frightening off the other person. The reason for this is there is an implicit understanding that the person receiving the disclosure feels it necessary to also disclose, and if the received disclosure is premature, then this could cause the other person to retreat.

CASE STUDY
Joe blows it!

Joe, in his early 20s, met Bill at the tennis club. They got along well and soon were arranging to go out for a drink. As they sat on the lawn of the pub, Joe told Bill that he was gay. Bill clammed up and was clearly uneasy. He made an excuse to leave.

Joe related this in a counselling session, as he explored what went wrong with his relationships. As we explored this latest incident he realised that he had told Bill about his sexuality hoping that Bill would tell him he, too, was gay. His answer to the question 'Why am I doing it?' revealed not a desire to be open but to push Bill into a relationship. Bill reacted by being scared off. While there was nothing for Joe to feel ashamed of in his sexuality, the disclosure was premature and wrongly motivated. His disclosure was bordering on manipulation.

> Be honest with yourself as to why you want to tell someone something.

IDENTIFYING THE GAINS AND RISKS OF DISCLOSURE

Disclosure is neither good nor bad; it has gains and risks, and the one has to be weighed against the other, though of course we will never know in advance how a disclosure will be received; whether it will be a gain or otherwise. If Joe had considered some of these pointers to gains and risks of disclosure, he might have developed a satisfying relationship with Bill.

Possible gains	**Possible risks**
Lessened loneliness	Rejection
Greater intimacy	Not liking self
More friendships	Feelings of shame
Self-responsibility	Being misunderstood
More assertive	Wary of confidentiality
Encourages disclosure	Feeling tense/vulnerable
Discovering others	Too much intimacy, too soon
Self-acceptance	Too many close relationships
Control of own life	Too much self-knowledge
	Breaking taboos about disclosures
	Balance of relationship disturbed.

When we are appropriately open we encourage others in appropriate disclosure, which enhances the relationship.

Using self-disclosure to develop relationships

- **Increase breadth and depth** of disclosures naturally as relationships develop.
- **Express feelings** appropriately (or not express them, but recognise and acknowledge them), not just talk about them.
- **Use immediacy**. Respond immediately and say what otherwise would remain unsaid.
- **Be genuine**. Let your disclosure be characterised by a willingness to let yourself be genuinely known.
- **Avoid questions**. Questions often avoid having to disclose. Too many questions can sound like an interrogation.
- **Learn to reciprocate**. Relationships can be prevented from becoming shallow by matching levels of disclosure, though not necessarily the details.
- **Use 'I' messages**. Recognising, owning and expressing your own feelings. 'I feel . . .' has more impact than 'One feels . . .'
- **Be specific**. Generalisations are too vague for people to relate to.

Reforming generalised statements as specific statements

Generalised: You don't love me.
Specific: When you come home from work, I would like you to kiss me.

Generalised: You never think about anyone but yourself.
Specific: If you know you're going to be late phone me. I worry about you.

Generalised: You're a male chauvinist pig.
Specific: I want you to listen to me while I'm stating my opinions, even if you don't agree.

Generalised: All you ever do is work.
Specific: I would like us to go to the beach next week.

Generalised: You never talk to me any more.
Specific: I'd like us to sit down together – with no TV – and talk for a few minutes every night.

Generalised: All parents think they know what's best for their children.
Specific: My parents think they know what's best for me.

What you can do to build self-disclosure skills
Be:

- direct
- sensitive
- relevant
- non-possessive
- brief
- selective.

Exercise 7.1   Owning your feelings
Before we can disclose feelings we must be aware of them, then we must own them as ours. In each of these questions you are invited to be open with yourself.

1 What feeling do you find easiest to express?
2 What feeling do you find most difficult to express?
3 Which person do you feel most at ease with?
4 Which person do you feel most uncomfortable with?
5 What is the thing you find easiest to do?
6 What is the thing you find most difficult to do?
7 Which one thing about yourself would you most wish to alter?

Do you want to own these feelings?
Would you be prepared for someone else to know this about you?

Exercise 7.2   Self-disclosure assessment
This assessment, which concludes the section on self-disclosure, presents a range of topics which some people may experience disclosing to others. As you work through the questions, relate them to one specific relationship.

I would share with . . . (give person's name):

1 My life goals.
2 How I behave when I'm angry.
3 Feelings of affection for someone.
4 Whether or not I cry when I'm sad.
5 My doubts and fears about life and death.
6 That I fancied someone.
7 My relationship with my parents.

8 How I think other people view me.
9 My feelings about someone being too dependent on me.
10 Some of the bad things that have happened to me.
11 Feelings about my sexual adequacy or inadequacy.
12 Any feelings of being isolated from people.
13 Guilt feelings, if any, I have (or have had) about sexual behaviour.
14 The parts of the body about which I feel inadequate or ashamed.
15 My feelings of disgust about someone.
16 Things in the past over which I feel ashamed or guilty.
17 My feelings about being dependent upon someone.
18 My feelings about being manipulated by someone.
19 The times when I've been dishonest.
20 The parts of my personality I most dislike and want to change.
21 My feelings of mistrust towards someone.
22 The times I've broken the law.
23 My feelings when I'm severely criticised.
24 The feelings I have about not being accepted.
25 Sexual dreams.
26 My worry about my emotional stability.
27 My feelings of prejudice towards the opposite sex or different races.
28 My thoughts about suicide.
29 My inner conflicts.
30 My feelings about being protective towards someone.
31 My feelings about situations when I've felt helpless.
32 My feelings about gambling.
33 The fear that I won't be a success.
34 The times when I've let other people down.
35 My feelings about my worth at work.
36 My feelings about the integrity of my performance at work.
37 My feelings of superiority.
38 The feelings I most have trouble controlling.
39 The times when I put on an act and am not myself.
40 The situations in which I feel afraid.

How honest were you with yourself? Being honest and open with yourself is the first step in being honest and open with other people.

EXPLORING VALUES IN RELATIONSHIPS

Values are the principles or standards which guide a person or society. Values are what we judge as valuable and important in life, or what we consider good or beneficial to our well-being. Values are learned beliefs, largely culturally determined, which show in our attitudes. As enduring beliefs values are part of our personality, and direct how we behave, think and, therefore, influence how we feel.

Values may be personal, such as honour, truth, freedom, education, the right to work, equality, the worth of life, of doing what is right and not doing what is wrong, of justice and fairness, and of honesty. These cannot be bought or sold, things can.

As with all aspects of personality, we do not hold one value to the exclusion of all others; but values exert a powerful influence on our lives. Values help to maintain and justify attitudes; the more value-relevant an attitude, the more resistant it is to change. Your values are an important part of your frame of reference, and opposing values are one of the major areas of internal conflict.

An important part of getting on with people is to explore your own values, for if there is one thing that will wreck a relationship it is a clash of values. Many of us take on our parents' (and others') values lock, stock and barrel, but part of developing self-awareness may mean engaging in the painful process of re-evaluating our values and maybe getting rid of some of them.

The process of evaluating and getting rid of outworn values never stops.

None of us is value-free. It is important, therefore, that we become aware of the influence our value-judgements exert. Being self-aware weakens our value-judgements so that they are less likely to act as emotional filters, which block the other person's feelings and dictate our responses.

CASE STUDY

Angela clashes with her boss

Angela and her husband, Keith, decided to give a party to celebrate Angela's promotion. They asked a number of their respective work colleagues, including Angela's boss and Keith's boss. Keith invited a work colleague, who asked if he could bring a partner. Angela and Keith both agreed. When they turned up at the party, it was obvious that they were a gay couple. Angela's boss drew her and Keith aside, and said, 'I'm not narrow minded, you understand, but I'm very surprised that you allow this sort of behaviour in your home. I run a well-respected company and I don't approve of this at all. I trust you will remedy it, now.' He turned to walk away.

Keith was bursting with indignation. Angela held onto his arm and moved alongside her boss, smiled sweetly and said: 'I know you do, that is why I like working with you. I respect your values, and I know you respect ours. At my interview you said you like to keep home and business separate, so I am sure you will respect that here. Now let me get you another drink.'

How would you have dealt with this? How would your values have made you respond?

Exercise 7.3 Identifying your personal values

This exercise (from my book *Self-Counselling*) is concerned mainly with personal qualities. Our belief systems and our values are deeply connected. We are motivated and make decisions based on these belief and value systems. Often these values are unconscious. We may not know why we choose to lie or stay honest, but we do.

The exercise can be applied in different ways, the choice is yours. Using the list of words below you may:

1 rank all the values listed
2 choose a certain number and rank those
3 or grade them as very important, important, less important. You may also use the words as triggers for a free association or imagery session.

nurturing	duty	obedience	security
ability	excellence	originality	self-realisation
outsmart	family name	peace	self-respect
acquisitiveness	friendship	physical fitness	service
affection	generosity	power	sex
ambition	happiness	privacy	status
appearance	honesty	professionalism	stubbornness
attractiveness	honour	religion	success

benevolence	independence	reputation	talent
character	integrity	respect	unselfishness
conventionality	intimacy	others	wealth
creativity	intelligence	revenge	youth

IDENTIFYING THE ORIGINS OF YOUR VALUES

1 Where did you acquire those values?
2 Are any of them now redundant in your life?
3 Are you being driven by someone else's values?
4 Do any of these values force you into unhealthy, stereotyped behaviour? If so, what can you do about it?

Exercise 7.4   Identifying values in relationships

The 15 statements listed below represent some of the fundamental values of close personal relationships. Relate every statement to yourself, and to a particular relationship that means a great deal to you. You may wish to add a few words about how and when you might react differently. Try to decide:

- Which of these values is essential in your relationships?
- Which of these values do you need to work on to improve your relationships?
- Are there any other values you consider important that are not included?

In my relationship with (insert the person's name) I try to:

1 Take responsibility for my own feelings, thoughts and actions.
2 Show respect by demonstrating that I accept and value her/him.
3 Show affection, liking and appreciation. I can both give and receive.
4 Show commitment to the relationship.
5 Show caring and concern for her/his total well-being.
6 Be open and revealing. I am trusting and prepared to take risks.
7 Feel safe to give and receive feedback, thereby helping each of us to stay open.
8 Avoid being defensive.
9 Avoid denying or distorting information in order to remain emotionally comfortable.

10 Show understanding through sensitive intuition, knowledge and effective listening.
11 Use anger by owning, understanding and handling it constructively.
12 Manage conflicts by not turning them into 'I win – you lose' encounters.
13 Avoid sexual exploitation, and work for mutual consideration and affection.
14 Share activities by allowing her/him time and space.
15 Spend time with her/him because our relationship is important to us both.

SUMMARY

Risk-taking is a significant factor in getting on with people, yet risk-taking does not come easily to all people. The ability to take risks is related to trust. Trust is the basis of relationships. Trust develops gradually and requires consistent and concentrated effort to maintain it. People who trust themselves generally find it easier to put trust in others.

Being open

An important area, linking risk and trust, is the ability to be open and to disclose one's self to others. It seems that by disclosing something about ourselves we will increase our vulnerability. In reality, the more open we can be the less vulnerable we become. Vulnerability is increased proportionate to the degree we hide behind our defences in order to protect ourselves from things which people can usually perceive anyway.

Risk, trust and openness are interlinked with how much we know ourselves. Self-knowledge may be enhanced by a degree of introspection and self-analysis, but also from being open to the feedback we receive from others.

8

Learning to Communicate Effectively

It is often difficult trying to decide where to place a chapter in a book. Learning is seldom achieved in neat parcels. Rather, various topics are inter-related. It is frequently the case that at the end of reading a book, we need to start it again to integrate what we have learned. Perhaps there is no easy way round this.

To get on with people, we must be able to communicate. This chapter introduces basic concepts and principles concerning the art and skill of communication. With so many misunderstandings happening between partners, couples, colleagues and friends, it is obvious that effective communication is not a natural attribute.

Meaningful communication is as much skill as art, and needs to be explained, understood and practised. As you work through the chapter, keep in mind: the more effective the communication, the more you and the other person will have the opportunity to 'hear' what each is saying. People can only 'hear' what we are saying when we communicate clearly and effectively.

As you read through this chapter, try to recognise where you yourself stand. What sort of a communicator are you? If you incorporate some of the skills discussed here, how will getting on with people be improved?

EXPLORING WHY WE NEED TO LEARN TO COMMUNICATE

We may think that as communication is so basic an activity we would all be experts. If that were the case, this book would probably never need to be written and you would not be reading it. It would be trite and inaccurate to suggest that all relationship breakdown results from faulty communication, yet there is sufficient evidence to suggest that if we learn to communicate effectively, one significant area of potential damage to relationships will be greatly reduced.

Identifying barriers to effective communication

Lack of trust
We can demonstrate lack of trust in subtle ways, such as asking a lot of questions, not hearing, changing the subject, hearing only the superficial message and not bothering to hear the feelings.

Misinterpretation
Sometimes what we say *is* misunderstood, but it is our responsibility to check it out and if necessary put it right. It is also our responsibility to check out that we have understood the other person's message. Assumptions form shaky foundations for relationships.

Stereotyped language
The greetings one gives along the street can be meaningless stereotyped responses. The over-use of endearments is another. A little boy was asked his name by his playgroup leader. 'Darling,' he replied. Puzzled at this rather unusual name, she listened to his mother as she talked to him. Never once in five minutes did she address Mark other than as 'darling.'

Emotional language
When we engage in highly emotive language, laying blame for example, we erect a communication barrier.

Intellectualisation
Sometimes we can speak in gobbledegook, or in jargon, or use such highbrow language that it may have the effect of causing the listener to feel stupid or ignorant. One of the great arts in communication is to say what you want to say in as few words as possible, and in language that everybody can understand.

Conceptual conflicts
Some people prefer to communicate in simple, concrete terms, black is black and white is white. Others prefer to communicate in abstract terms. Trying to carry on a conversation from these two different styles may create a great gulf which can prevent effective communication.

Cultural differences
Words, phrases and ideas of one culture are not always easily understood in another culture.

Exercise 8.1 Assessing your own communication barriers

1 From the seven barriers listed above, identify any that you experience difficulty with: why, and with whom and in what circumstances?
2 Recall a specific incident when you were not listened to. What were the facts? How did you feel? What led to your not being listened to?
3 Thinking about it now, how could you have put it right?

Questions to ask yourself about how you communicate
1 What can I do to create a conducive atmosphere, which is relaxed and comfortable?
2 Is this the best time to say what I have to say?
3 Is this the most appropriate place?
4 Am I adequately prepared?
5 Why do I want to communicate?
6 What does the listener expect?
7 How can I put the points over?

Identifying reasons for ineffective reception

- Lack of self-awareness. Do you think self-knowledge is a load of rubbish?
- Hidden agendas. Do you speak about something as a means to get at something else?
- Preconceived ideas. How open are you to change or to other people's ideas?
- Arguing. Arguments often veil a desire to dominate.
- Interrupting. You cannot interrupt and listen at the same time.
- Criticising. How often do you say 'I'm only saying it for your own good'?
- Putting down. Do you patronise people, desiring to elevate yourself?
- Not being able to get into the internal frame of reference. How often and how accurately are you able to see things through the other person's eyes?
- Distortion. Do you distort what is said to you? Can you identify who you are most likely to do this with? Can you identify your motives?

IDENTIFYING THE ELEMENTS OF VERBAL COMMUNICATION

Words themselves do not have meaning. Words are simply vehicles that we use for trying to convey something that has meaning for us, to someone else, in such a way that the receiver takes in our meaning. One of the difficulties with words is that we attach to them different experiential and emotional implications. Words are not always associated with similar experiences or similar feelings on the part of the listener and speaker.

Other difficulties encountered in using the verbal mode include the use of jargon, clichés and specialised vocabularies. It is often said that words have meaning only in context; it can be better said that words only have meaning when they are associated with people in context. There is no right way to say something. It seems that for many of us our experience is defined by our vocabularies and how we express ourselves – verbal fluency.

IDENTIFYING THE ELEMENTS OF NON-VERBAL COMMUNICATION

Non-verbal signals are often more valid than are words. Indeed, it is generally accepted that most of verbal language is conscious, while most of body language is at an unconscious level. Becoming aware of what the body – ours and other people's – is saying, is essential in effective communications. This does not mean that we become obsessed with 'people watching' but it does mean that we become aware of what the other person is saying.

For example: you are walking along the street and a stranger approaches you. You get ready to say 'Hello' but you don't. You walk past. Why? Did the person not make eye contact with you? Was there a slight movement of the body away from you? A slight tightening of the lips? A lowering of the head? Possibly all of these, or some of them, and because these signals were there, there was the clear message: don't talk to me.

Contrast this with your walking along the same street and some-one you know approaches, with head down. You say 'Hello' and there is no response. What goes through your mind? Maybe some-thing like this: 'Strange! Didn't she see me? Was there something wrong? She looked a bit low. She usually does speak. I must find out.'

Touching
Touch communicates a variety of potent feelings. Some of us give out body signals that say *'don't touch me!'* The person who gives

out signs of not wanting to speak is also saying 'don't touch me.'
Getting communication somewhere near right means respecting
all aspects of the other person. Some of us like hugs, other people
run a mile from them. Never assume that because you are comfortable hugging or kissing in greeting that everybody feels the same
way. How do you know? Is there a slight movement of the body as
you shake hands? Look for eye contact that says 'It's okay to kiss
me.' You may be forgiven for making one mistake, but if you go on
making the same mistake with the same person you run the risk of
the relationship withering.

Eye contact
We tend to size each other up in terms of trustworthiness through
reactions to each other's eye contact. Con men (and women) understand the importance of good eye contact, to convey trust and
liking. Counsellors convey understanding and acceptance, and become aware of what is going on in the client, through eye contact.
Speakers keep their audience interested by frequently looking
around. Salesmen watch for signs of a deal.

However, as with all aspects of communication, beware of making assumptions. People who don't make eye contact are not always shifty, in fact as the above example of con men shows, eye
contact might hide the truth. Some cultures find making eye contact very difficult. Learn what it is about the other person that
makes him or her unique and respect that uniqueness.

Space
We all have a psychological space around us. If another person
invades that space we may become tense, alert or closed up. We
tend to place distance between ourselves and others according to
the kinds of relationships that we have and what our motives are
towards each other. This psychological space relates very much to
touch and close contact. Some people find it easier to approach
another person than to be approached. Again, look for signs, particularly eye messages that say 'It's okay.'

Exercise 8.2   Assessing your own space
Knowing how much space you like is important in relationships.
Ask a trusted friend to help you. Get your friend to stand about
ten feet from you and walk slowly towards you. Maintain eye
contact. When you start to feel uncomfortable at the proximity,
ask your friend to stop. Take a rough measure of the distance.

Now reverse the exercise: you move towards your friend, and stop when you feel uncomfortable.

You may well discover that when you are passive you need a greater distance between you than when you are in control and moving towards your friend.

Your friend might like to participate in this exercise, and then you could compare notes. Doing this with a friend is of course different from the space you require with strangers, or with people of the opposite sex.

Finding out your different space boundaries is a useful exercise in self-awareness.

UNDERSTANDING FEEDBACK

The ability and willingness to communicate effectively is the key to success in relationships. One of the most important tools of maintaining control and developing people is **feedback**. It gives us the opportunity to be open to the perceptions of others.

Guidelines for giving feedback
1 Your intention has to be constructive, not destructive.
2 If feedback has not been requested, check if the person is open to receive it.
3 Deal only with observable behaviour, not with personality defects.
4 Deal only with modifiable behaviour.
5 Describe specifics, not generalities.
6 Make sure your desire is to help, not to punish.
7 Suggest, don't prescribe.
8 Do not make assumptions, or interpret. Let the person know the impact that the behaviour has on you.
9 Check for understanding.

Guidelines for receiving feedback
1 Try not to act defensively.
2 Try not to rationalise your behaviour.
3 Summarise your understanding.
4 Share your thoughts and feelings.
5 Accept responsibility for your behaviour.
6 Try to see things through the other's eyes.

7 Explore the feedback, don't use it as an excuse for attack.

8 Don't brush it off with misplaced humour or sarcasm.

9 Don't put yourself down, assuming that everyone else is correct.

10 Plan how you could use the feedback.

11 If it is hard to take, remember, you did ask!

Examples of feedback

- I like you.
- Your fists are clenched.
- You're angry, and that's okay.
- When you shouted, I felt anxious.
- When you called me 'son', I felt put down and small.
- I'm feeling angry at what I consider to be a sexist remark.
- Yesterday you said . . . I felt very angry, though I wasn't able to express how I felt. I needed to think how to say it.

Exercise 8.3   Convert generalisations into specific statements

One of the characteristics of positive communication is to be specific, and not to resort to generalities. This exercise contains three general statements. Your task is to make them specific. You will find some suggested answers at the end of the exercise.

1 I'm glad to see that your work is improving.

2 You're a very supportive person.

3 You're falling down on the job again.

Suggested responses

1 I'm pleased that you met every deadline in the last three weeks.

2 I appreciate your taking time to explain the contract to our new employee.

3 Last month most of your cost reports were completely accurate, but last week four of your profit/loss figures were wrong.

Recapitulation

- When you are *giving* feedback, report accurately the situation as you observe it.
- When you are *receiving* feedback, reflect what you think the other person meant, felt or thought.
- Feedback supports growth. The only way we can ever see ourselves as others see us is to take heed of what they tell us. We

must always bear in mind, however, that one person's view may result from faulty perception. When many people say the same thing, then it is time to sit up and take notice.

Exercise 8.4   Examining your communication

1 Think back over the last week and the communications you have had.
2 Identify *who* used feedback, and then identify how you felt about that feedback.
3 How many times did you give accurate and appropriate feedback? How do you think it helped the relationship?

CASE STUDY

James doesn't hit the right note

James, the office manager, was fed up with Ann. She is often late for work, and when she breezed in one morning with, 'Morning all' he snapped, and shouted at her and told her off.

The boss, who came in just then, said nothing but a few minutes later called James in and said 'When you snapped at Ann in front of the group, she appeared to be very embarrassed and angry. When you must remind an employee to be on time, it's less embarrassing for everyone to discuss it with the employee privately later.'

What did you think of the way the boss dealt with James?

EXPLORING LISTENING

- **Listening**   is *taking in* what is communicated.
- **Responding** is *giving out* what you want to communicate.

Listening and responding are two relationship skills. When was the last time someone really listened to you? When was the last time you really listened to someone else?

Identifying indicators of non-listening

- Advising, giving solutions.   *Why don't you . . .*
- Evaluating, blaming.   *You are definitely wrong.*
- Interpreting, analysing.   *What you need is . . .*
- Lecturing, informing.   *Here are the facts . . .*
- Name-calling, shaming.   *You are stupid.*
- Ordering, directing.   *You have to . . .*
- Praising, agreeing.   *You are definitely right.*

- Preaching, moralising. *You ought to . . .*
- Questioning, probing. *Why did you . . .*
- Sympathising, supporting. *You'll be okay. Don't worry!*
- Warning, threatening. *You had better not . . .*
- Withdrawing, avoiding. *Let's forget it.*

Identifying poor listening habits

Listening does not always come easily, neither is it constant. Our listening waxes and wanes, like the moon, depending on the situation and who we are listening to. We can become so used to someone's voice and message that our attention drifts and we only half hear. Here are some typical examples of poor listening.

- Not paying attention. Watching TV while your child is speaking to you.
- Pretend-listening. Looking at the speaker but your mind is miles away.
- Not hearing the meaning. Responding only to the facts.
- Rehearsing what to say. You want to get your point over.
- Interrupting the speaker in mid-sentence. What you have to say is more important.
- Hearing what is expected. You think you know what the speaker wants to say.
- Feeling defensive, expecting an attack. For example, the person might be angry and you anticipate the anger is directed at you.
- Listening for something to disagree with. Maybe you normally have to present the other side.

Responding as a part of listening

- Passive listening, without responding, is deadening and demeaning.
- We should never assume that we have really understood until we can communicate that understanding to the full satisfaction of the other person.
- Effective listening hinges on constant clarification to establish true understanding.

IDENTIFYING WHAT YOU CAN DO TO COMMUNICATE POSITIVELY

Try to get into the person's frame of reference; see things through the other person's eyes. Listen for total meaning – **content** and

feeling. They both require to be heard and responded to. In some instances the content is far less important than the feelings for which the words are but vehicles. We must try to remain sensitive to the total meaning that the message has to the speaker.

Being an active participant in communication releases energy, it does not drain it from the other person. Active participation is a process of thinking *with* people, instead of thinking *for* or *about* them.

COMMUNICATION CHECKLIST

Eye contact
- Do you look people in the eye when you talk to them?
- Do your eyes shift away when you are making an important statement?
- Are you able to maintain brief eye contact after you complete your statement?
- Do you lower your eyes when you are expressing negative feelings or saying No?
- Can you accept a compliment with full eye contact?

Facial expression
- Can you keep your face firm when you are expressing negative feelings?
- Do you feel uncomfortable when your face looks angry?
- Do you try not to let your face mirror your feelings?
- When you are happy to see someone, does your expression reflect the pleasure you feel?
- Do you avoid smiling or frowning because you are concerned about wrinkles?
- Do you find yourself smiling when you do not feel like it?

Tone of voice, inflection, voice volume
- Are you reluctant to use a firm tone of voice?
- Do you become uncomfortable around 'loud' people?
- Are you frequently ignored when you say something?
- Do other people interrupt you when you are talking?
- Do you frequently appeal to others in a childish voice, rather than expressing yourself assertively?
- Are you able to speak or ask a question in front of a large audience?
- Are you afraid to speak slowly?

Body stance
- Do you minimise your effectiveness by slumping or holding your head down?
- Do you freely use gestures to express yourself?
- Do you have difficulty knowing what to do with your hands?
- Do you antagonise other people with critical gestures?

Non-words
- Are you afraid of silences?
- Are you aware of non-words you frequently or habitually use?
- Do you interfere with your communication by excessive movements or sounds?

SUMMARY

Faulty communication creates stress between people and endangers relationships. Rather than take a purely abstract, theoretical point of view, apply the insights of this chapter to your own life. In what situations do you reckon you feel stressed because of the way other people communicate with you? On the other hand, how do you communicate with other people? What pressures do you put them under?

Communicating with people is both art and skill. We can develop both on our own, to a certain extent, by thinking about what has taken place and what is to take place. However much we may 'practise' on our own, there comes a time when we need to try it for real. Over recent years for example we have seen the development of the simulator for training airline pilots. There comes a time when the pilot moves out from the simulator into real life. So must we, who would be effective communicators. It might be possible to enlist the help of others to simulate communication, but there's nothing like the real thing. It takes courage, patience and persistence.

Being effective communicators
However we were raised, whatever the communication styles of our family, school, and so on, there are many 'bad habits' to unlearn and to be replaced with more effective ones. We did not learn to talk in a day; neither will we learn to be effective communicators without a great deal of hard work.

Effective communication depends upon being aware of how we communicate symbolically, verbally and non-verbally. We must also be able to give positive feedback and be able to receive feedback, without being defensive. On the other hand, negative feedback can be very destructive.

Communication would be a sterile exercise were it not for listening and responding; two sides of the same coin. Listening is far from the passive state which some people think it to be. Active listening – as it has been presented here – is a skill of great sophistication, which is available to all who would attempt to acquire and practise it. Active listening hears what is said between sentences and without words, what is expressed soundlessly, what the speaker feels and thinks. This listening and the responding that goes with it are born of the parents of self-knowledge and intuition, qualities which will enhance all your relationships.

I would like to be able to promise you great things if you improve your communication skills; if I did, you would suspect my motives, and rightly so. I would be judged to be not genuine.

Whatever you achieve, never let it be said of you that people couldn't get through to you because you didn't listen to them.

9

Exploring Personality in Relationships

There are many approaches to the study of personality. One is the work carried out by Carl Jung, and in the early 1940s expanded by Isabel Briggs Myers and her mother, Katherine Briggs, who began exploring ways to use Jung's theories to explain personality differences. Their paper-and-pencil instrument for determining personality type became known as the **Myers Briggs Type Indicator (MBTI)**. The highly respected MBTI is now used worldwide.

UNDERSTANDING THE MYERS BRIGGS TYPE INDICATOR (MBTI)

The four MBTI dimensions are:
- **Extraversion** (E)
- **Sensing** (S)
- **Thinking** (T)
- **Judging** (J)

- **Introversion** (I)
- **Intuition** (N)
- **Feeling** (F)
- **Perceiving** (P)

These are defined as follows:

- Extraversion: seeks stimulation from the outer world of people and things.
- Introversion: seeks stimulation from the inner world of ideas and thoughts.
- Sensing: perceives through the five senses; works with facts.
- Intuition: perceives through hunches; works with possibilities.
- Thinking: makes head judgements.
- Feeling: makes heart judgements.
- Judgement: influences decisions; creates order.
- Perception: influences decisions based on gathering information.

The MBTI classifies each person in one of 16 personality types, based on that person's preferences for one aspect from each of the four sets of letter pairs. For example ESTJ or the opposite, INFP.

David Keirsey and Marilyn Bates, in their book *Please Understand Me II*, use the same four dimensions found in the MBTI to outline four 'temperaments' – SJ, SP, NT or NF. (For readers who would like to add to their understanding of personality typing, *Please Understand Me* provides a detailed self-scoring questionnaire.)

The MBTI seeks to explain the central aspects of personality, to individuals themselves, to their co-workers, as well as to family, partners and friends. It describes the great variety of talents, and emphasises the ways in which some people are not just different from each other but opposite and complementary. Their strengths are our weaknesses and vice versa. Getting on with people has as much to do with temperament as it has to do with all the other qualities and skills discussed in this book.

Most of us have times when we become perplexed by having to relate to others who are quite different from us. Even the simplest tasks can be approached in different ways, causing confusion and misunderstanding, not to mention hurt and angry feelings. We can help ourselves and others to get on with people by a greater understanding of our different personality preferences.

The four personality preferences
- **Extraversion/introversion** is the way we relate to the world around us.
- **Sensing/intuition** is the way we perceive the world.
- **Thinking/feeling** is the way we make judgements.
- **Judgement/perception** is the way we make decisions.

By becoming aware of how preferences influence relationships, you can better understand each other's motivations and behaviours, and can expand tolerance and respect for each other.

Exercise 9.1   Assessing your basic preferences
From the description of the four dimensions, would you place yourself more:

E than I?	I than E?
S than N?	N than S?
T than F?	F than T?
J than P?	P than J?

Make a note of your assessment to refer to later.

How do you think your preferences influence who you are, what you do and how you relate to people?

SUMMARISING MBTI

Before continuing the discussion, it is essential for me to point out several important points about personality preferences.

1 They are not absolute; they are only guides to understanding certain parts of personality.
2 Everybody has elements of all eight preferences, though most of us prefer one of each pair over the other.
3 No one preference is inherently good or bad, positive or negative. All of them serve a purpose.
4 Always think of preferences as being 'more of one than the other' in every pair.

Dissimilarity does not mean inferiority!

Exercise 9.2   Assessing your temperament within relationships

If you are in an intimate relationship, invite your partner to do the same exercise you did (9.1) to assess your dominant temperament. When you have both made your assessments, discuss your findings and see if there are areas which lead to difficulty, as well as those that lead to harmony between you.

EXPLORING SOME GENERALISATIONS ABOUT PREFERENCES

1 People who have the same strengths in the dimensions will seem to 'click', to arrive at decisions more quickly, to be on the same wavelength. Their decisions, however, may suffer because of similar blind spots.

2 People who have different strengths in the dimensions will have difficulty getting on the same wavelength and may have difficulty accepting some views, opinions and actions of the other. Decisions arrived at from their interaction will, however, generally be more sound and more acceptable.

3 The parts of our dimensions we don't use much – the 'shadow' side – we are more sensitive about and more prone to react negatively when criticised about. As a result, conflict may occur when we must work with our shadow sides or when our deficiencies are pointed out by others.

4 We are generally attracted to people who display similar preferences. On the other hand we are often drawn to others because of the strengths we observe in them; the flip side of our own preferences.

5 Our values, beliefs, decisions and actions are all influenced by the four stronger dimensions of our typology.

6 Although our preferences are fixed, we can work with our shadow sides and strengthen them in order to overcome problems that result from the weaknesses.

CASE STUDY

A tale of Fred and John

John and Fred are business partners. John's MBTI type is ENFJ; Fred's is ESTJ. John and Fred arranged a meeting to discuss their plan for the following year. John gave it some thought, jotted a few ideas down on the back of an envelope, and waited for things to bubble away in his subconscious.

Prompt on the dot, John arrived at Fred's house, carrying a bundle of papers and books he thought they might look at. Fred, on the other hand, had meticulously prepared a programme, with everything spread in strict order around the table. A neatly drawn flow chart indicated the expected route of the discussion.

When they had been going for a few minutes, Fred said something that caught John's attention and reminded him of something among his papers. Fred asked to keep that until later; 'It'll throw me off my stride. Can't deal with tangents.'

Fred made notes as he went along, neatly appending them to his programme. Several times he drew out a diagram from his collection to illustrate a point. All his drawings and overhead transparencies were numbered and kept in order. Several times John said something like, 'What do you think they will feel about that?' to which Fred replied, 'If it's presented logically, they can't really argue, can they?'

Sometime during the meeting, after Fred had covered all his points, John said, 'Fred, I've written this article for the journal, will you proofread it for me. I know you'll dot the i's and cross the t's.'

Fred said, 'I need to think through an idea, here it is, what does it look like to you? What will the staff think about it?'

Discussion

John and Fred matched their E and J. Both liked working with people and were outgoing and worked well to deadlines.

Fred perceived the world through his S, and worked well with detail and needed to take his plan in a logical sequence.

John perceived the world through his N, and would have been quite happy, to let things roll and see what developed.

S and T often go together. Fred, though not insensitive to feelings, was more comfortable using logic to achieve his goal. John needed to take other people's feelings into account.

Fred needed John's N and F; John needed Fred's S and T.

From this short case study can you identify some of the ways you work with people? Now that you are aware of personality preferences, how do you think you might use this awareness to enhance your relationships?

STRIVING FOR HARMONY IN RELATIONSHIPS

(This section is based on *Please Understand Me II*, by David Keirsey and Marilyn Bates.)

Understanding the sensing perceptive partner

If your partner's type is SP, these are some guidelines to help you understand him or her.

- As with most other activities, sex for the SP is there to be enjoyed – to the full – now, not later. They respond to tactile, auditory and visual sexual stimuli.

- A relationship that develops with great speed may soon become a burden on the SP independent spirit. So, just as quickly, the relationship may end and the burden be discarded.
- The SP often operates on a short fuse, then it's back to normal. Confrontation, however, is difficult, the preferred course of action is to retreat into silence. When under pressure they can become very tactless or even cruel. This may also lead them to be insensitive to any harm they may have done.
- They are not good at arranging priorities and they are so caught up living in the present that they may overlook their obligations.
- The SP delights in giving and receiving gifts, often extravagant ones. Gifts may be at the expense of necessities; something which may irritate the partner.
- The SP has little respect for saving for the future. Living for today is central to the SP temperament. Money, sex, friends are all there to be enjoyed – now. They are often into the latest and the best.
- The SP finds an outlet for creativity in arts and crafts. Clutter does not seem to bother them. They are drawn to strong colours. Plants are likely to adorn every windowsill.
- SP parents expect, and get, obedience from children, though it is balanced with autonomy and freedom. They are not given to sentimentality.

The sensing judging partner
- The idea of enjoying or needing sex does not sit easily with the SJ. Sex is a service offered for security and comfort. Many injunctions surround sex not being 'the thing.'
- Purpose is important to the SJ. Children are there for the purpose of extending the family line. Family history is kept alive with stories and anecdotes.
- Affection is expressed in standard, almost stereotyped, ritualised ways. Gifts are intended to be treasured. Flowers fade and wilt, and will seldom be given.
- Possessions are significant, but they are valued for their usefulness and long-lasting qualities. They should be functional and without show.
- The SJ is careful with money; budgeting, planning well for the future, investment in insurance, bonds and savings accounts. Sacrifice now for benefit later.

- Home may assume a focus to the exclusion of all else. Spouse and children may become the reason for existing, life without them is unthinkable.
- Children are expected to toe the standard line. The SJ has a strong sense of right and wrong, and tends to see things in black or white terms.
- The SJ is the typical 'pillar of society'; involved in church, civic or community activities. Small talk is time-wasting and frivolous. Punctuality is a virtue.
- Life with an SJ is predictable, but safe. The same weeks of the year and the same place for holidays, going with the same like-minded friends.

The intuitive thinking partner

- The NT may appear cold, serious and unemotional. The intellect is likely to get in the way of sexual enjoyment. Public display of affection does not appeal.
- The NT wastes few words, and rarely states the obvious. This can lead to problems with the partner to be told, 'I would have thought it was perfectly obvious I love you.'
- If a relationship fails, the NT is just as likely to shrug it off as 'one of those things.' Once committed, however, the NT seldom looks back.
- The NT does not tolerate emotional conflict such as quarrels; debate and logical argument, yes, but acrimony is destructive. They will walk away from emotionalism.
- Spontaneity and play are difficult. Pleasure is in discussing abstract issues, playing around with words and their meanings. They are often offended by practical jokes.
- The pursuit of wealth rarely interests NT people. Possessions are accumulated not as symbols of status, simply to be enjoyed. They like to feel comfortable. The home of the NT is likely to be bulging with books, as representing knowledge. The partner may feel that the thirst for knowledge is at the expense of family priorities.
- The NT often needs to be reminded of birthdays and anniversaries. Family responsibilities are taken seriously. Parenthood is a pleasure, although they often give the impression of not being emotionally involved.

The intuitive feeling partner

- NF people are skilled in the art of romantic relationships. They respond with tenderness, sympathy and frequent passionate expressions of love. The partner of an NF will always feel that this is perfect love.

- Before marriage, both male and female NF are often totally blind to any flaws in the loved one. Later, the male NF can lose interest in the partner and continue his quest for perfect love.
- The female NF sees only perfection, rarely the flaws. For her, the main delight is to bring sexual pleasure to her mate. To fall in love once is a life-time fulfilment.
- They rarely forget birthdays and anniversaries, however they can be deeply wounded when people don't remember their milestones.
- The NF is naturally empathic, which can be both a strength and a weakness. Someone who has felt encouraged to become dependent may then feel rejected by the NF when suddenly told, virtually, 'Stand on your own feet.' This is not being unkind or callous; it is the only way the NF can handle such over-whelming dependency.
- NF people can become so overloaded with their own concerns that they find it difficult to cope with conflict or pain of those close to them.
- NF people often fail to organise priorities. The demands of other people may take precedence over family needs. NF people are always seeking new relationships, which may be at the ex-pense of those already established.
- No other type has the same capacity for empathic understand-ing, and a relationship with an NF holds the promise of warmth, appreciation and support.

Exercise 9.3   Assessing you and your best friend

Taking the descriptions of four temperaments: sensing perceptive, sensing judging; intuitive thinking; intuitive feeling:

1 Where would you place yourself?
2 Where would you place the most significant person in your life?
3 What is it that makes for harmony between you?
4 What is it that makes for friction between you?
5 What do you think you might be able to do to decrease friction and increase harmony?

Exercise 9.4   Getting on with people at work

1 Think of a situation, either at work or in your private life, where you had to work closely with someone.

2 What preferences can you identify which helped your collaboration?

3 What preferences can you identify which hindered your collaboration?

UNDERSTANDING PREFERENCES AND COMMUNICATION

Es: may feel under pressure to do all the talking – for themselves and for Is.

Is: may feel ignored by Es who are often more willing to enter a conversation and keep it going.

Ss: may feel irritated by Ns who jump to conclusions – sometimes correctly – without working through obvious stages.

Ns: may feel irritated by the caution of Ss who, to them, often take a long time to arrive at conclusions.

Ts: may feel irritated by Fs who do not approach a problem logically, and want to talk about how they feel.

Fs: may feel irritated by Ts who want to analyse everything with cold logic before making a judgement.

Js: may feel irritated by Ps who never seem to be able to make a decision and always want to put things off and put play first.

Ps: may feel irritated by Js who insist on having everything planned, won't let things just happen and insist upon work first.

Exercise 9.5   Assessing communication style

Taking the preferences and communication from above as your base line, think of a relationship in which you are currently involved.

1 From the description of different styles of communication, where would you place yourself? Where would you place the other person?

2 How many of the characteristics outlined are you able to identify with that cause you irritation?

3 What characteristics of yours do you think might cause others to be irritated?

4 Now that you have been introduced to how personality preferences might influence the way people communicate, can you

identify what sort of people annoy you most? Which do you feel more at harmony with?

5 Having carried out this assessment, how has it helped you understand yourself and other people a bit more?

SUMMARY

The proposition of this chapter is that personality and temperament certainly play an important part in how two people get along. Again, however, it must be emphasised that just achieving a match between personality types does not automatically guarantee compatibility any more than, say, marrying a person with a compatible star sign would. There is more to successful relationships than horoscopes and the MBTI.

That being said, misunderstanding and friction, resulting in relationship stress, often do arise from the different people:

- relate to the world – (E/I)
- perceive the world – (S/N)
- make judgements – (F/T)
- make decisions – (J/P).

My intention was to show that we often act the way we do because we have different programmes running and sometimes these bring us into conflict with other people.

It would be tempting to believe that all problems are caused by incompatibility of preferences. But that would be like saying that all road accidents are caused by drunk drivers. While there is a certain truth in that statement, it is not the whole truth.

Working with differences

Opposites can live in harmony as much as people with similar preferences can get on really well, *provided they accept each other – warts and all!* When a couple have opposite preferences they have the wonderful opportunity of complementing each other and creating a complete whole of two distinct parts. Learning to live in relative harmony and balance and, at the same time, drawing on the strengths of one's partner, is an effective way of reducing relationship stress.

People who are too extraverted often get on people's nerves; someone who is too introverted often has difficulty making contact with people at all.

People who are high on sensing can get so caught up in counting the trees that they miss the beauty of the wood; people who are too intuitive often seem 'away with the fairies'.

People who are too high on thinking often intellectualise everything; people who are too high on feeling often swamp others by their warmth.

People who are too high on judgement often become judge, jury and executioner; people who are too high on perception often give the impression of being grown up children.

Effective relationships might require you to work towards making changes in the way you relate to the world; how you perceive the world; the way you make judgements; and the way you make decisions. Even small changes can work wonders.

If your spouse, partner or someone else with whom you relate closely is your opposite, you have a wonderful opportunity to experience more about yourself.

When you accept the parts of yourself that you don't pay much attention to, because you prefer other parts, you acknowledge that perhaps there are potentials there lying dormant, and that leads to greater well-being and wholeness.

Acceptance, remember, is a special kind of loving that transcends sexual attraction and sexual activity. Sex does not last for ever, acceptance develops with time.

Let the person you most closely relate to teach you about yourself, and he or she will, if you accept his or her personality preferences.

10

Handling Relationships Under Stress

The more intense the relationship, or the more intimate, or the longer it lasts, the more chance there is of stress developing. People who only meet casually or infrequently, or who meet only for a specific purpose – such as tennis partners – may experience some tension but it will not be the same as, for example, the tension and stress between husband and wife or in other close relationships.

LOOKING AT HOW TENSIONS DEVELOP

Falling in love, or engaging in a new relationship, is exciting and occupies much of our time and emotional space. The chemistry buzz is wonderful and thrilling. Sex between couples in love can transport both into realms of bliss. But the feeling of falling in love cannot last; otherwise you would forever be falling through space. Falling in love is gradually replaced by 'being in love', an entirely different experience. Here is where the marriage vows of: in sickness and in health, for better or for worse, for richer or for poorer, become reality.

I know that many couples have not gone through such a marriage ceremony, and are as deeply committed to each other as those who have. The ceremony is not the point: committing one's self to another person *as a life-long partner* is, and demands the same degree of care and compassion as stressed in the marriage ceremony. What greater evidence of love than to be with another person throughout all of life's trials and tribulations, as well as in all of life's blessings?

However much a couple are in love, tensions do develop and if these are not resolved they will lead to a build-up of stress, which can grow to such an extent that it drives the couple apart.

> Learning what creates so much stress that it could lead to breakdown of the relationship is essential in keeping the relationship alive.

This is not a book about stress or stress management. However, the book would not be complete if it did not examine the possibility that relationships can create stress, and stress can seriously affect relationships. Stress, as distinct from pressure, affects our general health and well-being. If these are affected then the logical result is for relationships to suffer.

Exercise 10.1   Identifying your stress levels

This section covers six potential stressors between you and your spouse/partner, or other significant person. The items are not conclusive, they can only point to what *could be*, not to *what is*.

Answer every statement with:

1 Is this a stressor for us?
2 On a scale of 1 (no stress) to 5 (high stress) rate each item for your marriage/partnership or other significant relationship.
3 The action we can take to reduce the stress is . . .

(A)   Problem-solving and decision-making
1 One of us always ends up giving in to the other.
2 We stop each other from growing.
3 We can't agree on what we want out of the marriage.
4 We don't seem to understand each other's point of view.
5 We don't seem to be able to solve problems together.
6 Minor difficulties often turn into great crises.

(B)   Child-rearing
(If you have no children, how was it with your own parents? And what influence does their experience have on you today?)

1 We disagree on what, and how much, the children should do around the house.
2 We disagree on what morals the children should be taught.
3 We disagree on how children should be disciplined and punished.
4 We disagree on how much children should be praised and rewarded.
5 We disagree on what spare time the children should have and how they use it.
6 We disagree on what the children should and should not do.

(C)   Relatives and in-laws
1 One or other of our parents interferes by telling us how to run our lives.

2 Relatives quite often do or say things in public that embarrass us.
3 Our respective parents do not approve of our marriage.
4 We are dependent on our parents for financial support.
5 We often criticise each other's family.
6 Relatives are too ready to offer advice that hasn't been asked for.

(D)   Personal care and domestic arrangements
1 We disagree on how the home should be furnished.
2 We annoy each other by criticising each other's appearance.
3 We annoy each other by criticising each other's physical characteristics.
4 We annoy each other by criticising each other's state of personal hygiene.
5 We annoy each other by picking on each other's personal mannerisms.
6 We disagree on how and where to spend our holidays.

(E)   Money matters
1 We rarely consult each other before spending money.
2 We disagree on how much to spend and how much to save.
3 We often have arguments about how much each spends, and on what.
4 We live beyond our means, and can't agree on how to change it.
5 We were in debt when we married, and can't get out of it.
6 We spend too much on some luxuries at the expense of necessities.

(F)   Friendships and affection
1 One of us always tells the other not to show too much affection in public.
2 One of us would like to be more open with affection when in public.
3 One of us is involved sexually with someone else.
4 One of us objects to the friends the other one has.
5 Neither of us is really interested in what happens to the other during the day.
6 Neither of us wants the other to have relationships outside the marriage.

Interpretation
(This is a rule-of-thumb interpretation, not a 'scientific' one.) If you have more than two in any section that scored 4 or 5, what can you do to reduce the stress levels?

Very high: 144-180. Your relationship is certainly under great strain. You need skilled professional help. Seek it at once, both of you, if your relationship is to survive.
High: 143-108. Your relationship is under strain, and things are likely to get worse unless you take action *now*. You may find it helpful to talk your problems through with a counsellor, colleague or a trusted friend.
Medium: 107-72. While your relationship is under some strain, you are still on the right side of the track, but should guard against complacency. You and your spouse/partner probably have a lot of talking to do.
Low: 71-36. Like everyone else, your relationship has its ups and downs, but you can normally work things out amicably. Take a close look at the individual stressors, perhaps there you will find something to work on to enhance the relationship.
Very low: 35-0. Your are either to be congratulated at having achieved a near-perfect relationship, or you have not answered the questions truthfully! Is your relationship really the ideal, or is it just plain dull? Are you two saints living in perfect harmony? If you have answered this without consulting your spouse/partner, it might be revealing to get her/him to do it and compare the findings.

HIGHLIGHTING THE STRESS OF INTIMACY

Intimacy is like a harp. The music it produces comes from all its strings. Intimacy means discovering the particular harmony and melody that is enjoyed by the people involved. Sometimes the melodies will vary. Sometimes a minor key will be more appreciated than a major one. (Source unknown)

Defining intimacy
In general terms, intimacy means the state of being closely familiar with another person, not necessarily of the opposite sex and not necessarily sexual. Intimacy with at least one other person is generally regarded as an essential ingredient of a healthy and satisfying life. It is thought that intimate relationships are an essential

component of human well-being, and that their absence causes distress.

The absence of an intimate relationship, the inability to share emotions, to trust others or make a commitment to a stable, lasting relationship, is often a significant cause of mental and/or physical distress and an indication of an intimacy disorder. The capacity for intimacy fosters self-worth and a feeling of belonging. Many people, of either sex, have difficulty talking about intimate matters.

Some people imagine that sex is being intimate, and that the more they engage in it, the more fulfilled they will be. However, sexual experiences by themselves cannot create intimacy or fill the void or boost his or her self-esteem. Mere repetition of the sexual act no longer satisfies. There is a deep hunger for intimacy which can only be found in a relationship of commitment. People who fail to develop the capacity for intimate relationships run the risk of living in isolation and self-absorption.

ENHANCING INTIMATE RELATIONSHIPS

Of course there is no such thing as the ideal relationship! However, that does not prevent us from trying to better what we have got. As you work through the list below of things which can enhance your relationship, apply it to yourself. Try to be as honest as possible. You might care to add to the list of things you consider to be important.

Ways of enhancing your relationships
- Have fun.
- Love each other no matter what.
- Be willing to work through conflicts.
- Encourage each other's abilities.
- Co-operate and work together, and try to avoid competing with each other.
- Respect each other.
- Express and talk about your feelings.
- Be willing to negotiate and compromise.
- Take note of and celebrate accomplishments – small and great.
- Feel secure enough to make mistakes.
- Feel secure enough to say 'I was wrong.'
- Listen, really listen, to each other.

- Share resources equally.
- Be affectionate and warm, but never intrusive.
- Respect each other's right to privacy.
- Avoid disagreements at mealtimes.
- Respect and encourage individual differences.
- Make it okay to cry.
- Be honest with each other but respect the need not to disclose.
- Strive to be courteous and considerate.
- Be loyal to each other, and never run the other person down to other people.
- Care for each other.
- Aim to build each other up.
- Try to avoid making assumptions about what the other is feeling.
- Be totally committed to each other.
- Give and take quite freely in the relationship.
- Try to avoid blaming the other when things don't go right.
- Try to empower and encourage each other.
- Try to be real at all times.
- Try to avoid subjects you know offend.
- Give each other whatever space and time they require, without feeling ignored.

Add your own items.

GUIDELINES FOR REDUCING RELATIONSHIP STRESS

I am indebted to the Institute of Counselling – see Useful Addresses – for permission to use this section from their Introduction to Stress Management course, Lesson 6.

- Remind each other that you are on the same side.
- Communicate to be heard, not to win.
- Remember, it is not your job to teach your mate right and wrong.
- Don't confuse compliance with caring, nor lack of compliance with lack of caring.
- Don't assume that because your partner does not tell you every day that he or she loves you that love has died.
- Principles are rarely more important than people. Find room for both!

- Make requests, not demands.
- *Ask* for what you need. Don't wait for your partner to develop mental telepathy!
- Put yourself in your partner's place and help each other understand how you see things.
- Perfection is unique; go for compromise.
- Jealous feelings denied will operate as underground saboteurs.
- Learn to work within each other's frame of reference.
- Give yourself permission to relax.
- Speak for yourself.
- Be good to yourself.
- Know yourself as you are, not as you think you should be.
- Don't look to your mate to compensate for your parents' inadequacies; and don't try to parent your partner.
- Know that you can put yourself in your partner's hands, both literally and figuratively.

Advice: No matter how much effort we put into trying to understand the dynamics of a relationship, we may not be able to alter behaviours and expectations that are firmly entrenched or operating on automatic pilot.

If problems seem to be unyielding, couples counselling may be just what you need to help you pinpoint the sources of stress and heal a troubled relationship.

USING PERSONALITY PREFERENCES TO AVOID WORK STRESS

One of the factors which leads to stress in relationships, particularly where people live together, is work. Stress at work often spills over into home life, and where both partners are working they each bring their own stress into the relationship.

Understanding something about personality preferences and work is one way in which you can support your partner and help to defuse stress levels. It must be emphasised that the weakness of one preference is often moderated by the strength of another preference.

Summary of personality preferences and work

- **Extraverted** people working in an office by themselves will normally find this stressful. This is because the extraverted part of us needs frequent contact with people. **Introverted** people working in a job such as sales will normally find this stressful. This is because the introverted part of us needs plenty of space and time to think without interruption.

- **Sensing** people who are required to write complicated reports would find the task stressful. This is because the sensing part of us likes to move swiftly from fact to fact without long explanations. **Intuitive** people would find a detailed job such as accounts stressful. This is because the intuitive part of us finds it difficult to cope with too much detail.

- **Thinking** people who are expected to work with emotional problems that have no logical solution would find this stressful. This is because dealing with feelings puts the thinking part into conflict. Feelings are often irrational. **Feeling** people would find the impersonality of being a computer operator very stressful. This is because there is no communication with the computer.

- **Judging** people would find it stressful to be in any job that did not have clear-cut rules to work to. This is because without clear guidelines the judging part of us feels lost. **Perceptive** people would find the pressure of a newspaper, with its deadlines, very stressful. This is because the perceptive part of us would feel too controlled.

Where there is a mismatch between types and jobs it could be deduced that some people will not feel satisfied. If that dissatisfaction reaches a critical point, stress will result and may show itself in absence from work.

However, as in all aspects of life there are no hard and fast rules. Much will depend on the strength of the dominant preferences, and the degree to which the person is able to put that preference onto 'hold' and get on with the job. Another factor is how much use the person is able to make of external influences to achieve a balance.

Exercise 10.2 Assessing the compatibility of your work and preferences

1 If you are currently working, or have worked, how did your preferences influence the type of work you chose to do?
2 If you experienced stress at work, how much of it was due to a clash of preferences?
3 If you are experiencing stress at work now which is related to preferences, what can you do to reduce your stress levels?

4 How do you think your personality preferences influence your most significant relationship?
5 Overall, what do you think you have learnt from this discussion on personality preferences and types?
6 What do you think you might be able to do to lessen stress in your most significant relationship?

CASE STUDY

Vicky and Charles complement each other

Charles was a college administrator, a job which demanded a great deal of attention to detail. His personality type was ENFJ, which meant that he liked to be with people, and this was fine as he was able to get out and about and meet people. He was intuitive, and he made the most use of this in creating new systems, based on visual display. His thinking and feeling functions were almost 50/50, and this suited him very well. He needed to have a clear brain, yet be able to meet people at their feeling level. His judging function was very high, so he worked well with deadlines and enjoyed creating pithy and well-structured reports.

When he moved into the post his assistant, Vicky, was in almost every respect the opposite. She was introverted and slightly aloof. Her sensing function was highly developed, and her previous work as a bookkeeper made the most use of that function. She was a thinker, and could argue with Charles and present a logical case. Like Charles, Vicky was high on judgement and preferred working to deadlines. Their work was so well organised that they were hardly ever caught out. Their plans were worked out months ahead and rarely went wrong. Neither had any problems making decisions. It was generally acknowledged that they ran a tight ship.

Vicky was unmarried, and her private life was kept very private. Charles was married to Pat, and here there could have been difficulties. Pat, like Charles, was more extraverted than introverted, but very high on sensing, feeling and perception, and low on intuition and thinking. Her type was ESFP. She was certainly not unintelligent (and people who are low on thinking can give that impression) but her feeling preference (much higher than Charles's) meant that debate and discussion, which Charles liked, were difficult for her. Ask her to handle a difficult relationship problem and her input was spot-on. Charles found this difference easier to cope with than the other two differences – sensing and perception.

Pat was not content with Charles's broad details of something; she had to have *all* the facts; all the nuts and bolts. If Charles was relating a conversation, Pat had to know *precisely* what was said, and in what order. Charles was irritated by this attention to detail, just as Pat was irritated by his lack of detail. Lack of detail made her anxious, and she could not move forward until all the detail was there.

Pat had never grown up! At heart she was still a child, adorable, fun-loving and irritating to Charles when he needed to be serious. Pat was a tease, and while this was one of the characteristics that had attracted him when they were courting, as they grew older his own inner child was suppressed while hers continued to flourish, a fact that endeared her to all the children in her care at the playgroup.

Charles and Pat attended only one counselling session, arranged by mutual consent, to talk about the stress they were feeling in their relationship. On listening to them, I was struck by what I have outlined above. Pat was sad that they didn't have fun any more, and Charles was irritated that it took ages for Pat to get ready to go out, and she dithered and found it difficult to make up her mind.

We worked through the MBTI and it was wonderful to see the light dawn on both of them. We looked at the areas in which they agreed. In many ways they complemented each other. What was strength for Charles was weakness for Pat; and vice versa. If they pooled their resources they would have an overflowing emotional bank balance. That is what they did. I met them by accident about one year later, and in the supermarket aisle we chatted for a few minutes. Charles said, 'I now ask Pat if I've given enough detail.' Pat said, 'I now ask Charles to give me a five-minute time-check when we're going out. We hardly ever quarrel now.'

Understanding what makes your partner tick is a sound foundation for working together to relieve a build up of stress.

SUMMARY

Long-lasting and intimate relationships are prone to experience stress. To take marriage as an example, when the excitement and thrill of being in love is replaced by loving and life settles into a well-established routine, then is the time when stress develops. When children are added to the equation, there is added stress.

Although children were not discussed they bring their own tensions, and unless the parents are firmly rooted in each other children can drive a wedge between them. When children are reared in a shaky parental relationship they sense the tensions and experience their own stresses.

Some couples come into marriage with the idea that they can change the partner in some way. Attitudes and beliefs are notoriously difficult to change, so are habits. Change will happen gradually and naturally, but it can never be forced or demanded. People who love, want to please each other, but there has to be a balance between pleasing because you want to and pleasing because you feel manipulated into doing so. A relationship with that as the motive will result in disharmony. People who love each other do grow to be like each other.

Dealing with stress in a relationship

Stress can come from many sources, but if the relationship is to succeed the couple must find a way of handling the stress without it wrecking the relationship. There is no easy way, and no iron-clad blueprint either for avoiding stress or coping with it. We all must find our own strategies. However, if we recognise some of the ways in which stress can develop, we are part-way to dealing with it. Some of the exercises in this chapter will help you increase your awareness of what might be creating stress in your relationship. In the next chapter we shall look specifically at problem-solving as a way of helping to reduce stress levels.

Finally we again looked at the place of personality preferences as they relate to work. From my experience as a counsellor I conclude that the majority of people will cope with stress at work provided they have a relatively stress-free relationship at home. Conversely, people who are experiencing stress at home will cope, provided stress is not piled on them at work.

> When there is stress at home *and* at work, that is when the emotional knees start to buckle.

11

Handling Relationship Breakdown

None of us enters into a relationship with the idea that it will break down. We hope it will last for ever. Sadly that is often not the case. Most of us invest heavily in relationships that are significant to us, and the thought of separation is something we choose not to contemplate.

If you have reached a stage in some significant relationship where it looks as if it will end, is it too late to try to repair it? I wish I could offer cast-iron reassurances that it was not, but I can't. Certainly I have seen damaged relationships repaired, but it requires a great deal of willingness on the part of both people, and sometimes one or both people have become so hurt that the willingness to repair the damage is not there. Facing the inevitable breakdown may be all you can do, at the same time maintaining your self-esteem and self-confidence. The closing pages of this book are offered as a way to develop a problem-solving strategy to help you work through a severed relationship.

COPING WITH A SEVERED RELATIONSHIP

Pain, feelings of grief and loss are experienced when a relationship is severed. The more we invest in a relationship, the more intense, intimate and long-lasting the relationship, the more intense these feelings will be.

Severance may mean death, or divorce, but it can also mean losing one's job, either through redundancy or retirement. Although this book does not deal specifically with the workplace, in this context it is pertinent, for severing of work relationships can be extremely traumatic.

Dealing with divorce

If death is the final parting, divorce is the spectre that haunts the living, with rattling chains of what once was and might have been. The intimate relationship knot is easily tied, and with the passing of time the knot bites deep. The cutting of the knot is not achieved without leaving deep scars.

Divorce is death of a relationship. People who suffer the breakdown of an intimate relationship experience the full range of feelings similar to those experienced when a death occurs, with one crucial difference, the 'ex' is still around. In many ways the grief can never be wholly resolved; a bit like when a loved one is drowned at sea and the body is never recovered. Or like many thousands of relatives whose loved ones died during war and their bodies were never found.

Problem-solving

In this the final chapter I offer some hints on problem-solving. Some people are natural problem-solvers; others are not. Learning that there are definite steps in solving problems might help you to avoid a breakdown in your relationship. However, all the strategies in the world might not put right what is threatening the relationship, and the relationship may come to an end.

One of the characteristics experienced as we contemplate a severed relationship is that our thoughts and feelings fly around in confusion. We find it difficult to focus on constructive action and we may feel that we are in danger of losing our grip on life. Problem-solving might be too much of an effort. Yet just focusing on some definite steps can help you to get your feet back on firm ground.

GETTING TO GRIPS WITH YOUR PROBLEM

Problem-solving is goal-directed, aimed at improving a situation or resolving a conflict. When difficulties remain unresolved, we may experience symptoms such as anxiety and depression. Problem-solving is one way of relieving stress. Focusing on a model, such as follows, makes use of your thinking function, and doing so temporarily puts your feeling function on hold. Try it when you are next beset by feelings that fly around like frightened chickens in a coop when disturbed by a marauding fox.

WHAT YOU CAN DO TO AID PROBLEM-SOLVING

- Have a healthy **self-respect**, which means accepting your own personal worth and what you have to offer.

- Have a healthy **other-respect**. This may mean giving credit to those who think differently. It also means being able to listen to what others say.
- Develop a healthy **optimism** that problems can be solved if everyone is willing to work at them to find an acceptable solution.
- Try to develop a **respect** for, but not fear of, conflict. Let the conflict create something better.
- Develop a **willingness** to invest energy and to take risks.

IDENTIFYING COUNTER-PRODUCTIVE BEHAVIOUR

Counter-productive behaviour includes:

- Denying the problem exists.
- Ignoring it, hoping it will go away.
- Blaming something or someone for it.
- Blaming yourself. While it is healthy to take some of the responsibility for a breakdown in a relationship, taking all the blame is probably not realistic and turns you into a victim.

WORKING WITH THE NINE-STAGE PROBLEM-SOLVING MODEL

1 Define the problem.
2 Decide a method of attack for the problem.
3 Generate alternatives.
4 Test alternatives for reality.
5 Choose an alternative.
6 Plan for action.
7 Implement the plan.
8 Evaluate.
9 Follow-up.

Step 1 – define the problem

- What precisely is your present difficulty? For example: I have been divorced; my wife has died; I have lost my job.
- Identify precisely your thoughts and feelings. For example: I feel betrayed; angry; lost.
- Who is doing what, to whom?

- Are my perceptions accurate?
- Is communication distorted?
- What is at stake?
- What decisions do I have to make, and when?

Step 2 – decide strategies

- Is there anyone else who can help?
- Do I need any more information? If so, what? You may not know until you start exploring.
- Do I know anyone else who has successfully solved this problem? For example, if you have been divorced, or lost your job, how did other people cope under similar circumstances? But do remember, however others coped your situation is different, but try to learn from them and adapt their experiences to suit you and yours.
- What resources can you tap? For example, if you have been widowed find out what singles clubs are available, if that suits you, or what advice is available to help you through the early stages. A call to your local CAB office will help.

Step 3 – generate alternatives

- **Brainstorm**, if possible with someone else. Brainstorming is a method for generating ideas, simply by jotting down ideas, without discussing them or evaluating them. When you consider there are no more ideas, then start to explore them in detail.
- Think through each alternative, looking at positive and negative aspects.

Step 4 – test alternatives for reality

- Don't eliminate possibilities too quickly.
- Prepare a **detailed response**, by generating at least three positive statements about an alternative.
- Consider rejecting an alternative only when you have worked out a detailed response.
- Try operating the detailed response before rejecting something.
- Work out a 'for' and 'against' for each possibility.
- When all possibilities have been filtered through the detailed response, arrange them in a hierarchy of feasibility. This means arranging them from the least likely to the most likely, then make a decision to concentrate on the most feasible.

Step 5 – choose an alternative
- The chosen alternative must be within your capability and within available resources.
- Focus on the goal, then use imagination to generate new alternatives.
- Brainstorm how to weaken restraining (negative) forces, and how to strengthen facilitating (positive) forces.

Step 6 – plan for action
- Choose a plan that is appropriate to the potential solution. There is a danger of becoming so engrossed in the planning that you lose sight of the original problem, or the alternatives.
- Brainstorm what could go wrong.
- Rate each potential problem in terms of **probability** on a 1-10 scale. For every item rated above 5, allow a **threat** rating. A rating of 10 would mean catastrophe.
- If you cannot prevent the problem, how can you minimise its effect?
- Write a plan that takes account of:
  - tasks, what needs to be done
  - responsibilities, who needs to do what
  - deadlines, which part needs to be completed and by when.

Step 7 – implement the plan
- Begin simply, and gradually. Take one step at a time. Build brick by brick. Take time to stop and take stock. Don't rush in blindly.

Step 8 – evaluation is at two levels
- The first level is an evaluation of the action plan itself; how far did the plan meet your set goals and objectives? It may be necessary to go back to step 6.
- The second level evaluates how effective the overall problem-solving was. Just how far did the plan contribute to the outcome?

Step 9 – follow-up
- Follow-up is essential. If the original problem still exists, use **5Wh** – Kipling's 'five honest serving men': what, why, when, where, who and how. What succeeded; what did not? Why did it succeed; why did it not? When was the best time; when was the worst time? Where did I get the best information; where the

least helpful? Who helped the most; who gave the least help? How can I make the most use of what I've done?

- It may be necessary to go back to stage 1 and repeat the process.
- Follow-up may also be helpful to consolidate the learning experience.

ESSENTIAL PROBLEM-SOLVING SKILLS

1 Active listening, clarifying, paraphrasing, self-disclosure.
2 Diagnostic skills (steps 1 - 2).
3 Decision-making skills (steps 2 - 5).
4 Data-collecting skills (steps 5 - 6).
5 Design and planning skills (steps 5 - 8).
6 Organising/administrative skills (step 7).
7 Analysis skills (step 8).

HELPFUL HINTS TO COPE WITH A SEVERED RELATIONSHIP

Do not:

- withdraw from life
- deny the way you feel
- back away from relationships
- put yourself down for feeling vulnerable
- be surprised at sudden physical problems
- dwell on the unfairness of it all
- base relationships entirely on trying to please
- rush into another relationship, whatever your circumstances
- make visits to children a series of spectaculars if you have been divorced
- indulge in guilt about sometimes being away from children.

SUMMARY

Analysing relationships is a bit like telling someone how to breathe or how to walk. Breathing and walking are so natural that we hardly ever think about them. Only recently I visited someone in hospital, where I saw a young man walking with a frame, assisted by a physiotherapist. 'Think what comes next,' the physio said. 'Put your weight on the frame, then your left foot . . .' and so on. This young man had injured his back while swimming; now he was having to *relearn* how to walk. Possibly for the first time since he was a few months old, he was having to think about what he was doing. I am certain that he will never again take walking for granted.

So it is with relationships. They are part and parcel of our day from waking to sleeping, so why do we need to *think* about them? Perhaps having worked through this book you will be able to answer that question with more insight than when you started it. The old Yorkshire saying 'Nowt so queer as folk' is true, and of course we are all tempted to say, 'Not us; we're okay.' We may say it with tongue in cheek, for we all have much within us that irritates ourselves, let alone other people.

Breakdown in relationships is a major source of damage to well-being and self-esteem. There is no blueprint for effective relationships. We all have to do the best we can in spite of our many limitations.

It could be argued that some individuals have 'people' gifts and qualities in dealing with others. Some people do seem to have natural relationship qualities, but they also have had to work hard to perfect those skills. An analogy may point home the message. The Wimbledon star did not arrive there only on talent alone; a great deal of dedication and hard slog were also necessary. Relationships are something like that.

Learning about relationships

Relationships may not be your forte but you cannot help but be involved with people. Learning about relationships is one way of increasing self-esteem. For every point won we increase the 'self-esteem-o-meter', and the more energy we shall have to enjoy life, and other people will feel the benefit.

If you and whoever else is involved have tried to keep your relationship alive but it ends up being severed, try using what you have learned in this book to help you towards healing.

Many people have never risked loving another person. Let the fact that you have loved bring its own rewards. Try not to let bitterness rule you.

Try to learn from your experience so that someone else might learn from you. In that way what you have experienced will be put to good use.

Glossary

Acceptance. The feeling of being accepted as we really are, including our strengths and weaknesses, differences of opinions, or whatever, no matter how unpleasant or uncongenial, without censure. It is not judging someone from a pre-determined set of values.

Active listening. Accurate and sensitive listening to the verbal and non-verbal messages which indicates to the other person that you are truly listening and taking in what is being communicated.

Affection. The need within a relationship to feel able to offer and receive love appropriately and in context.

Attitude. A pattern of more or less stable mental views, opinions or interests, established by experience over a period of time. Attitudes are likes and dislikes, affinities or aversion to objects, people, groups, situations and ideas.

Availability. Where we make ourselves emotionally available to another person. It demonstrates our willingness to be involved.

Brainstorming. Generating a free flow of thoughts and ideas that might help to solve a particular problem.

Confidentiality. Maintaining trust with another person by not knowingly passing on information, either facts or feelings, that have been entrusted to you.

Conscious. The content of mind or mental functioning of which one is aware. It involves perceiving, apprehending, or noticing with a degree of controlled thought or observation.

Control. The need to feel appropriately in control in a relationship, without either feeling the need to dominate or be dominated.

Distress threshold. The level of stress above which breakdown often results. Stress builds up until it reaches the threshold, then spills over as distress, affecting all aspects of the person's life.

Empathy. The action of understanding, being aware of, sensitive to, and getting in touch with the feelings, thoughts and experience of another, from either past or present, without becoming the other person.

Extraversion. The personality preference that moves out towards people.

Feedback. An essential mechanism in any interpersonal communication. It gives one person the opportunity to be open to the perceptions of others. Giving feedback is both a verbal and a non-verbal process where people let others know their perceptions and feelings about their behaviours. Without effective feedback, communication will flounder.

Feeling. The personality preference which relies on making heart judgements.

Frame of reference. Hearing and responding in such a way that you demonstrate that you are trying to see things through the other person's eyes.

Genuineness. The degree to which we are freely and deeply ourselves, and are able to relate to people in a sincere and undefensive manner.

Inclusion. The need to establish and maintain satisfactory relations with people; to feel included.

Individuality. The willingness to relate to people as unique individuals.

Introversion. The personality preference which draws inwards towards self.

Involvement. The degree to which we can become emotionally involved in a relationship.

Insight. In psychological terms, the discovery by an individual of the psychological connection between earlier and later events so as to lead to recognition of the roots of a particular conflict or conflicts.

Intuition. The personality preference which takes in information through hunches, rather than facts.

Judgement. The personality preference which relies on rules and structure.

Judgementalism. Where we judge people according to our own self-imposed standards and values, and impose them in a way that condemns and criticises.

Myers Briggs Type Indicator (MBTI). A paper-and-pencil personality test which measures eight preferences: extraversion/introversion; sensing/intuition; thinking/feeling; judgement/perception.

Openness. How prepared we are to let other people see beneath the surface; to let them be appropriately aware of our feelings, secrets and innermost thoughts.

Perception. The personality preference which relies on taking life as it comes.

Primary relationships. Long-lasting relationships, founded upon strong emotional ties and a sense of commitment to each other. An example is the parent/child relationship.

Problem-solving. Helping someone, or ourselves, to resolve some difficulty by working to a model or plan, the aim of which is to generate positive action.

Secondary relationships. More casual and short-lived than primary relationships, and with less emotional involvement. An example would be the relationship with the next-door neighbour.

Self-awareness. Self-awareness means being aware of our thoughts, feelings and behaviour, as influenced by our traits, values, attitudes, motives and memories, and the effect these have on other people.

Self-determination. The supposed right and practice of a people to achieve self-government, closely related to the concepts of nationalism and the nation-state. When applied to people, it is the person's right to act on the strength of one's personal beliefs and values rather than be coerced by what other people think is appropriate.

Self-disclosure. Where we disclose personal facts or feelings to another person.

Self-esteem. A confidence and satisfaction in oneself, self-respect. Self-esteem is the value we place on ourselves. A high self-esteem is a positive value; a low self-esteem results from attaching negative values to ourselves or some part of ourselves.

Sensing. The personality preference which takes in information through facts and details.

Spontaneous. This refers to how spontaneous we are in relationships, or how restrained we are in how we express ourselves.

Stress. An imprecise term, but generally taken to mean a state of psychological tension produced by the kinds of forces or pressures (stressors) that exert force with which the person feels unable to cope. The feeling of just being tired, jittery, or ill are subjective sensations of stress.

Thinking. The personality preference which relies on head judgements.

Trust. Confidence and faith in our own integrity and that of other people with whom we relate.

Unconditional regard. A relationship quality where we demonstrate total acceptance. It is a non-possessive caring and acceptance of the other person, without strings attached.

Unconscious. The part of the psychic apparatus that does not ordinarily enter our awareness and that is manifested especially by slips of the tongue or dissociated acts or in dreams. It is a reservoir for data that have never been conscious (primary repression) or that may have been conscious and are later repressed (secondary repression).

Values. Learned beliefs that we consider good or beneficial to our well-being and which influence our behaviour, thoughts and feelings and how we relate to people.

Warmth. One of the essential qualities in relationship-building. For warmth to be genuine, it must spring from an attitude of friendliness towards others. It feels comfortable; is liberating, is non-demanding.

Further Reading

A-Z of Counselling Theory and Practice, William Stewart (Nelson Thornes, 1997, 2nd edition).

Building Self-Esteem: How to replace self-doubt with confidence and well-being, William Stewart (How To Books, 1998, 2nd edition 1999).

Controlling Anxiety: How to master your fears and phobias and start living with confidence, William Stewart (How To Books, 2000).

Families and How to Survive Them, Robin Skynner and John Cleese (Mandarin, 1990).

Gifts Differing, Isabel Myers Briggs (Consultant Psychologist Press, 1980).

How to Solve Your Problems, Brenda Rogers (Sheldon Press, 1991).

Human Relationship Skills, R. Nelson-Jones (Holt, Rinehart and Winston, 1986).

Interpersonal Underworld (The), William Schutz (Science and Behaviour Books, 1966).

Learning to Counsel: How to develop the skills to work effectively with others, Jan Sutton and William Stewart (How To Books, 1997).

Learning to Thrive on Stress: How to manage pressures and transform your life, Jan Sutton, (How To Books, 1997).

Life and How to Survive it, Robin Skynner and John Cleese (Mandarin, 1994).

Making Marriage Work, Margaret Grimer (Geoffrey Chapman, 1987).

Please Understand Me II, David Keirsey and Marilyn Bates (Prometheus Nemesis Book, 1998). Kiersey provides a detailed self-scoring questionnaire.

Peoplemaking, Virginia Satir (Science and Behaviour Books, 1972).

Rebuilding: When your relationship ends, Dr Bruce Fisher (Impact, 1993).

Self-Counselling: How to develop the skills and the insights to positively manage your life, William Stewart (How To Books, 1998).

The RELATE Guide to Better Relationships, Sarah Litvinoff (Vermilion, 1992).

Useful Addresses

Association for Post-Natal Illness, 7 Cowen Avenue, Fulham, London
S26 6RH. Tel: (020) 7386 0868.
British Association for Counselling, 1 Regent Place, Rugby, War-
wickshire CV21 2PJ. Tel: (01788) 578328.
British Association of Psychotherapists, 37 Mapesbury Road, London
NW2 4HJ. Tel: (020) 8452 9823.
British Association of Sexual and Marital Therapists, PO Box No
13686, London SW20 92H. Tel: (020) 8543 2707.
Centre for Stress Management, 156 Westcombe Hill, London SE3
7DH. Tel: (020) 8293 4114.
CRUSE (Bereavement Care), Cruse House, 126 Sheen Road, Rich-
mond, Surrey TW9 1UR. Tel: (020) 8332 7227.
Depression Alliance, 35 Westminster Bridge Road, London SE1 7TB.
Tel: (020) 7633 0557.
Institute of Counselling, Clinical and Pastoral Counselling, 6 Dixon
Street, Glasgow G1 4AX. Tel: (0141) 204 2230. In addition to many
distance learning counselling courses, the Institute offers Psychology
for Counsellors, and an Introduction to Stress Management which
includes a relaxation instruction tape.
Institute of Family Therapy, 24-32 Stephenson Way, London N1 2HX.
Tel: (020) 7391 9150.
Miscarriage Association, Head Office, c/o Clayton Hospital, North-
gate, Wakefield, West Yorkshire WF1 3JS. Tel: (01924) 200799.
National Council for One Parent Families, 255 Kentish Town Road,
London NW5 2LX. Tel: (020) 7267 1361.
RELATE Marriage Guidance, National Headquarters, Herbert Gray
College, Little Church Street, Rugby CV21 3AP Tel: (01788)
573241.
Samaritans (for your nearest branch consult your local telephone
directory).
United Kingdom Council for Psychotherapy, 167-169 Great Portland
Street, London W1N 4HJ.

Index